DISCOURSES ON HISTORY SERIES
NUMBER 2

MAIN STREET IN THE EIGHTEEN SEVENTIES AND EIGHTIES
&
A BUSINESSMAN'S REMINISCENCES OF FIFTY YEARS

by Thomas Richmond Burrell Sr.
(1861-1953)

FALL RIVER HISTORICAL SOCIETY

Edited and annotated by Michael Martins and Dennis A. Binette

FALL RIVER
HISTORICAL SOCIETY
PRESS

Fall River Historical Society Press
451 Rock Street
Fall River, MA 02720
fallriverhistorical.org
(508) 679-1071

For information, write us at Fall River Historical Society,
451 Rock Street, Fall River, MA 02720.

LIBRARY OF CONGRESS CONTROL NUMBER: 2019938178

ISBN-10: 0-9641248-0-7
ISBN-13: 978-0-9641248-0-6

Printed in the United States of America on acid-free paper.

Book and cover design by Stefani Koorey, PearTree Press, Westport, MA

Front cover: View of South Main Street looking north toward City Hall, circa 1874.

MAIN STREET IN THE EIGHTEEN SEVENTIES AND EIGHTIES
&
A BUSINESSMAN'S REMINISCENCES OF FIFTY YEARS

When the Lusitania was sinking and Charles Frohman knew that he was facing death, he said: "This is the great adventure." But death is not the greatest adventure, death is the common heritage of man, the prince and the pauper, the miser and the spendthrift, the saint and the sinner, the wise and the foolish all, all at last limited to the six feet of earth.

The greatest adventure is not death but life, life with its boundless opportunities. Who would limit the possibilities of life?

Thomas Richmond Burrell, 1941

Contents

LIST OF ILLUSTRATIONS

INTRODUCTION TO
DISCOURSES ON HISTORY

At the time of its incorporation in 1921, and for the half century that followed, it was customary for members of the Fall River Historical Society (FRHS) to research papers for presentation at the organization's meetings. Traditionally, copies of these manuscripts were deposited at the FRHS, with the intention that they be made available to researchers, and a select few were serialized, in part, in local newspapers.

Not all of the lectures were illustrated at the time of their original presentation. The earliest of those that was accompanied by images featured black-and-white glass lantern slides, usually shown at the culmination of the lecture, while those of later date included slides in vivid Kodachrome. Fortunately, many of these images were donated to the FRHS, along with the original manuscripts.

In 1927, the organization published *Fall River Historical Society: Proceedings of the Society from Its Organization in 1921 to August, 1926*, which contained a selection of ten "papers on local subjects," and a comprehensive list of all of the speakers and topics presented as of that date. The volume was not illustrated, excepting one photograph of the Market Building and Town Hall, a solid Greek revival style building erected in 1845 of native granite. If the original intent was to publish additional volumes, this never came to fruition.

In subsequent years, the collection of papers amassed by the organization grew accordingly; topics varied widely, encompassing all manner of subject matter, with the common thread being the history of Fall River and its environs. This thematic variety furnishes a richly diverse tapestry, with subjects ranging from Native Americans to intrepid gold-seeking "Forty-Niners," from transportation in all its forms to industry of myriad types, or from memories of languid "Golden Summers" to the reminiscences of a policewoman, serving at a time when few women ventured into the field.

And what of the writers? Many individuals possessed superior literary skills and were methodical in research and writing, while others, somewhat less eloquent, nonetheless made the attempt, presenting papers on subjects that held their particular interest. The diverse personalities of the writers oftentimes come to the fore: There were those who pontificated, and others that rambled; some were witty, and others dry; and if truth be told, a few produced manuscripts that were accurately described by the transcriber of these papers as quintessential "yawners."

Among the presenters were brilliant conversationalists, and those with keen, descriptive memories; their papers are peppered with fascinating anecdotes, and references to individuals referred to by diminutives of their given names that would otherwise have been lost to history. So, too, were there academics, attorneys, ministers, physicians, and businessmen, whose oratory characteristically reflected their education and professions: the first lectured; the second deliberated; the third preached; the fourth delivered clinical narrative; and the last, board-room discourse or gentlemen's club banter.

Spinsters, of which there were several, often reflected through the lenses of proverbial rose-colored glasses, optimistically pining for Fall River of old and the halcyon days of their youth. Their nostalgic reminiscences served, perhaps, as an antidote for unfulfilled dreams and the oftentimes harsh realities of the "modern" world as they knew it; Fall River's cataclysmic economic decline, the Great Depression, and the horrors of two World Wars decidedly unpleasant topics.

Yet the vast majority of the papers produced have real substance, and at the core of each of them is the author's unmitigated passion for a particular subject. In many cases, the individuals who took pen to paper, or pecked away at typewriting machines, personally experienced the events of which they wrote, producing first-hand accounts with a narration little adulterated by the passage of time. Through personal reminiscences or those of their contemporaries, and with the aid of diaries, letters, and manuscripts then held in private collections, and now, perhaps lost, we are furnished with a glimpse of another age; the veil of time is lifted. Thus, the importance of these manuscripts cannot be understated; they are, indeed, compelling works, historical gems worthy of publication.

In some instances, the choice of words mimics the ideology and vernacular of the time, and may not be politically correct in the world of today; one must take into account the era in which they were written, and critique accordingly.

In addition to papers written in decades past, select contemporary works may also be included as part of the *Discourses on History* series.

In concluding one of the addresses in this volume, Fall Riverite Thomas Richmond Burrell Sr. (1861-1953) uttered a statement that epitomizes the objective of the *Discourses on History* series:

> And if I in writing this imperfect paper, if you in listening patiently to its reading, if the Historical Society in placing it with its records, have lifted these names from the list of forgotten men, I feel with you, that we are well repaid.

Indeed, if the publication of these manuscripts brings this to pass, the efforts of these long dead recorders of history has been validated; if they have once again been given voice, the Fall River Historical Society has fully met its objective.

Michael Martins
Curator
Fall River Historical Society

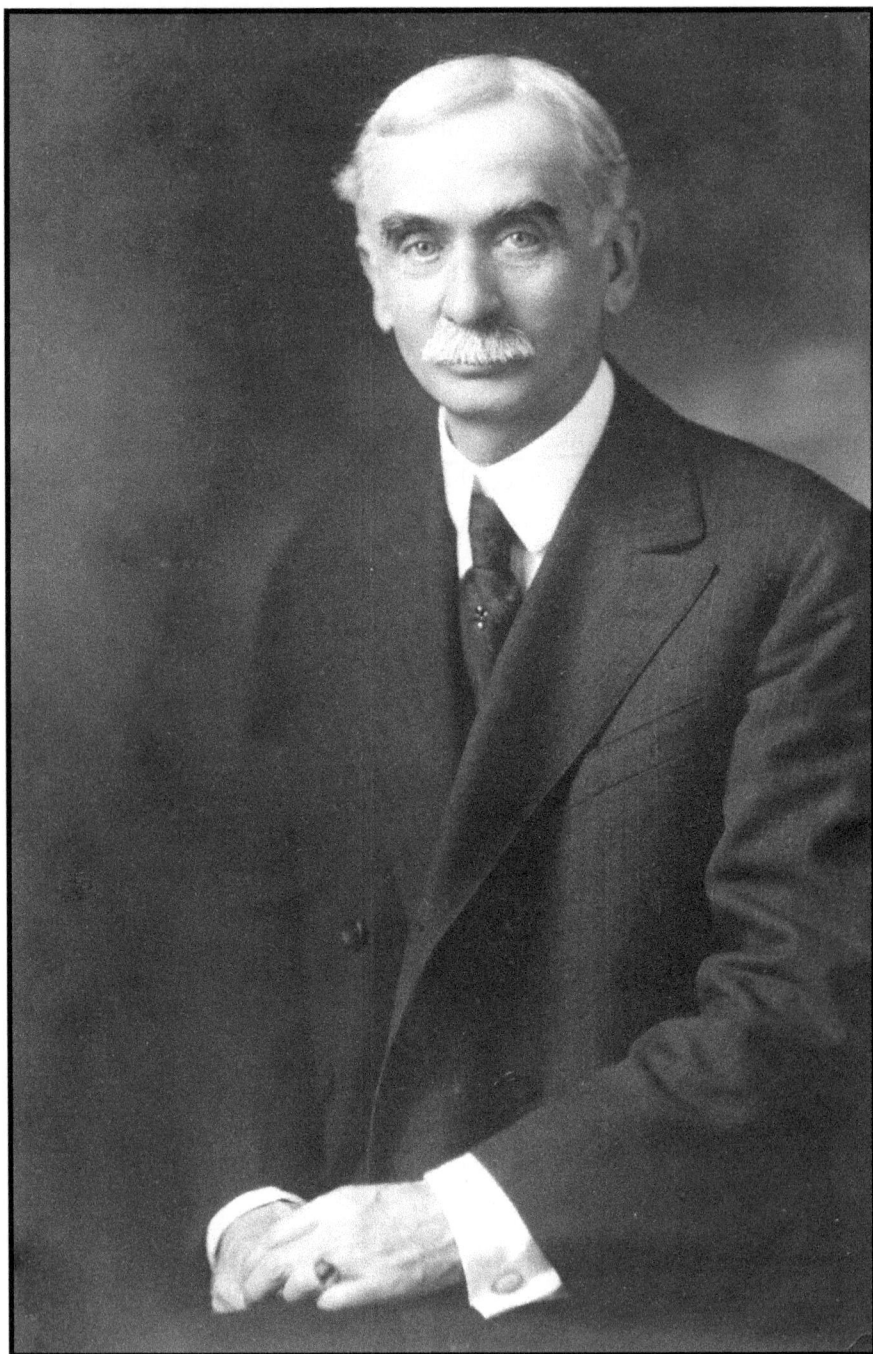

1. Thomas Richmond Burrell Sr.

About the Author

In 1943, a contemplative Thomas Richmond Burrell Sr. offered sage-like words of advice to a group of young men at their graduation ceremony:

> "You boys are just opening the pages, turn each one carefully, you will find every new page more interesting than the last."

For Burrell, these words were steadfast and true, and in many ways stood as testament to the long life he had enjoyed: Indeed, he had lived by them.

Thomas R. Burrell was born in Fall River, Massachusetts, on September 18, 1861, the third of the seven children of John Bates Burrell (1826-1883), a harness-maker, and the former Elizabeth Fales Richmond (1828-1919). His siblings were: John Thaxter Burrell (1857-1904); Mary Richmond Burrell (1860-1932), later the wife of Charles Gifford; Robert Carver Brown Burrell (1863-1936); Charles Bates Burrell (1867-1906); Leah W. Burrell (1870-1963), later the wife of John J. Maloney; and Miss Clara V. Burrell (1872-1959).

The Burrell children were descended from illustrious New England stock and could trace their ancestry directly from John Carver (1576-1621), writer and first signer of the Mayflower Compact and the first Governor of Plymouth Colony.

At the time of Thomas' birth, the United States was torn apart by war, and his native city on the verge of its greatest era of economic prosperity; Fall River would quickly gain acclaim as the Spindle City, a power-house of textile manufacturing and America's leading producer of cotton cloth - in fact, one of the leading textile producers in the world.

In time, Thomas would interact with many of Fall River's leading industrialists and other key players in the business and civic communities on a near-daily basis, gaining a unique personal insight into the prodigious business acumen possessed by some of the city's grandees, as well as their personalities, peculiarities, and, in some cases, their peccadillos. So, too, did he know and interact with the shopkeeper, the politician, the clergy, and the common man-on-the-street.

Perhaps unknowingly, much of this interaction was seared into his extraordinary memory, allowing him decades later to conjure up "out of the distant past" a "flood of memories ... grasping one here and there as they whirled through [his] mind." As these scenes played out in thought, as they once had in reality, and "slowly ... approached and passed from [his] vision," they flowed, ink-like, to his descriptive pen as he put thought to paper.

Thomas was educated in the public schools of his native city and often told his family that as a boy he was seated behind Lizzie Andrew Borden (1860-1927) in grammar school; this scenario is highly plausible, with students arranged in the alphabetical order of their surnames.

He completed his education at the Fall River High School, graduating with the class of 1878. Sixty-five years later, in 1943, he recalled the words spoken by the gentleman who presented his diploma, which by that time was, "a small roll of paper, yellow with age, tied with a faded blue ribbon, the writing almost invisible":

> We do not give diplomas to those who fail, we give them
> only to those who succeed. We do not praise those who
> fail, only those who succeed.

Throughout his life, Thomas exemplified this sentiment.

Fall River's rapidly thriving economy funded the expansion and reconstruction of much of its downtown business district and Thomas witnessed, first hand, the demolition of many of the small, old-fashioned stores of his youth, as they were replaced with modern, far more imposing structures.

Among them was the construction of the Borden Block, a massive edifice that was built on the site of several smaller buildings in a choice location, bordered by South Main, Pleasant, and Second Streets. Fall River's leading commercial block was an elegant red brick and sandstone structure that housed storefronts, two lecture halls, myriad offices, artist's studios, and the acclaimed Academy of Music, an opulent state-of-the-art theatre that boasted the second largest stage in New England.

The Academy of Music opened to the public on the evening of January 6, 1876, with a grand concert by the celebrated Theodore Thomas

Orchestra. The gala was a major social event of that season and was eagerly attended by members of the city's leading families, with all the "house attendants [*being*] prominent young men of the city."

The opening was a milestone for fifteen-year-old Thomas, who remembered it "so distinctly" for the rest of his life. He "had charge of the coat room," and was astounded when the ever-extravagant Charles Pickett Stickney (1824-1902), a prominent Fall River businessman – later imprisoned for embezzlement – "handed [*him*] Mrs. Stickney's [*Mary Anna Stickney née Davol*] fur coat with a dollar tip. The boy "had never heard of tips before and [*he*] never forgot that one."

Decade's later he wrote:

> After the performance we were all invited by the management to [*George*] Tallman's Restaurant in the [*Merchant's House*] basement on South Main Street. I had never eaten in a public place of that character before and I can taste that oyster stew now. But I had a guilty feeling all the while as to the approval of my parents who were strict Methodists.

In 1878, Thomas entered the employ of the Fall River National Bank, where he worked as a messenger at a salary of $150 per year; thus began his diverse seventy-five-year business career. Astute, honest, and hardworking, he soon rose through the ranks of the "Fall River National," and was appointed Teller, a highly-responsible position that, in the banking industry of the era, held a more prestigious connotation than the occupation today.

His ability to multi-task was remarkable and throughout his life he simultaneously held positions with various business concerns, at each of which he excelled.

On December 4, 1883, he married Mary Elmira Worth (1862-1942), a native of nearby Acushnet, Massachusetts, and a resident of Fall River; the service was conducted by the bride's father, Rev. William Tallman Worth (1834-1903), and witnessed by her mother, the former Sarah A. Gee (1836-1895). The year before, in October, 1882, Thomas's elder brother, John T. Burrell, had married Mary's older sister, Fanny Kent Worth (1860-1928) – thus the brothers were brothers-in-law, and the sisters, sisters-in-law.

Thomas and Mary were the parents of two children: Grace Worth Burrell (1885-1971), who later became the wife of Richard Herbert Bennett, and Thomas Richmond Burrell Jr. (1889-1965).

By 1885, Thomas had accepted the dual position of agent of the

Borden Block and theatrical manager of the Academy of Music, the latter then recognized as one of New England's leading theatres; its stage played host to many of the most illustrious American and European actors and actresses of the day, who performed their greatest roles to an enthralled Fall River and regional audience.

Thomas' days at the Academy and his interactions with various thespians – some of whom became friends, among them Edward Hugh Sothern (1859-1933), Julia Marlowe (1865-1950), and Henry Denman Thompson (1833-1950) – were later documented in his paper, "The Academy of Music in the Old Days," delivered before the Fall River Historical Society in 1939. Unfortunately, the present whereabouts of the extensive theatrical scrapbook he compiled during that period, containing clippings, personal memorabilia, and photographs, is unknown.

During his Borden Block years, he also pursued other business interests: From 1885 to 1887 he was associated with his brothers, John and Charles, in the aptly named Burrell Brothers, a book and stationery shop on South Main Street; and, in 1888, he served as treasurer of the Edison Electric Illuminating Company.

By 1890, he had entered the insurance business in Fall River and, the same year, moved his office to Boston, Massachusetts; he and his family resided in Boston, and, later Dorchester.

Thomas returned to Fall River by 1895, and for the next several years was associated with the State Mutual Life Insurance Company, in the capacity of general agent. At the same time, he pursued a writing career, working as Financial Editor for the *Fall River Daily Globe*; in the latter, his interest in the city's textile industry came to the fore and, as he perceptively witnessed its ebb and flow, he became an authority on the subject.

His astute business ability and keen "judgement in financial matters" brought recognition in the greater Fall River community, which he served in various capacities over the years, among them: President of the Algonquin Printing Company, the Flint Mills, and the Stafford Mills; vice-president and director of the Luther Manufacturing Company; and as a director of the Merchants Manufacturing Company.

Involved in civic affairs in Fall River, he was a member of the Board of Registrars of Voters, serving several stints as chairman. Erudite in fiscal affairs, he was appointed chairman of the Board of Assessors, a position "he filled with distinction." In all, he gave "about seventeen years of service [to] the city," working in various capacities.

In about 1903 he entered the field of outdoor advertising when he became associated with firm of E.E. Manchester & Co., Bill Posters and Distributors, as co-owner; the next year, he became sole proprietor. Thomas served as treasurer and remained actively involved in the newly-formed Fall River Poster Advertising Company until his death; the firm remained in his family for three generations.

Active socially, he was passionate about the history of his native city and was a long-time member and director of the Fall River Historical Society; he was one of its most popular lecturers, and it was noted that his papers "served to perpetuate the history of Fall River." When he was being introduced as a speaker by the secretary of the organization, his talks were habitually complimented with the words: "All of those who have heard Mr. Burrell's former papers will know what an interesting evening is in store for them."

He was involved with several advertising associations throughout New England, and was the national director of the Outdoor Advertising Association of America; headquartered in Washington DC, the trade organization had been founded in 1891. A proponent of social welfare, he was also affiliated with the Steven's Home for Boys in Swansea, Massachusetts, and served as its president for several years.

Active fraternally, he was an officer and Past Master of the King Philip Lodge AF & AM [*Ancient Free and Accepted Masons*], and at the time of his death was the oldest living member of that organization. In 1937, he was presented with a fifty-year medal on behalf of the Grand Master of the Grand Lodge of Massachusetts; the presentation was made by his son, Thomas R. Burrell Jr., who was also a Past Master of the Lodge. Likewise, some years earlier, Burrell Jr. had been presented with "a Past Master's jewel" by his father, Burrell Sr.

In fact, membership in the organization was very much a family affair; Thomas' brother, John T. Burrell, was a fellow lodge brother and had also served as Past Master.

On the evening of April 22, 1941, Thomas was asked to introduce Honorable Christian Archibald Herter (1895-1966), Speaker of the Massachusetts House of Representatives, who was making a presentation as guest speaker for a King Philip Lodge membership event. During his introduction, Thomas spoke of his long-standing affiliation with the Lodge:

> I thank you for this greeting and it reminds me of an old Irish gentleman, a janitor, who I met in the bank a short time ago. He called me over and waving a check said, "Mr. Burrell, for thirty years I have brought me pay check

every Thursday, the bank has never said they were short, or asked me to wait a few days, they always have adequate reserve to take care of me checks. Isn't that a pretty good institution to be connected with for thirty long years?"

So I feel that there is always an adequate reserve of good feeling, and I may say, affection, in this Lodge for me. Isn't that a pretty good institution to be connected with for fifty-four long years?

And for your information and perhaps relief, this is the last check that I expect to draw upon this reserve.

At a period in life when the vast majority of his contemporaries had long since retired – or died – Thomas remained actively engaged and interested in business, civic, fraternal, and national affairs. Very much a product of Fall River, he matured and prospered with it; in tandem, as youth progressed to middle, and then old, age, he bore witness to its dramatic economic decline; despite this, his optimism and love for his native city – and his joie de vivre – never wavered.

He was also a devoted family man.

Insight into Thomas' habits and personality can be gleaned from the childhood recollections of his great-granddaughter, Martha MacKay (Burrell) Foster, who resided with her family at the Burrell house during World War II; she has treasured memories of the man she always called "Great Father."

Among those recollections: The "always impeccably dressed" Great Father's daily routine of eating "stewed prunes for breakfast"; his twice-daily habit of winding the "clock that stood on the landing of the stairs"; his gift of her first tricycle that Martha "rode on his porch"; and his "adored white dog, 'Fleury,'" that appeared in photographs seemingly as often as family members. Best of all, was frequently "sitting on his lap" as "he told … stories and poems."

A favorite was a parody of the 1826 poem "Casabianca," by Felicia Dorothea Hemans (1793-1835); the poem was indispensable in nineteenth-century elementary school reading books, and Thomas undoubtedly had been made to recite it in his youth. The version he recited to his great-granddaughter, however, was delivered tongue-in-cheek, and would not have been acceptable to any of his former spinster schoolteachers:

The boy stood on the burning deck,
And he was all a quiver,
He had a cough, his leg fell off,
And floated down the river.

In 1941, Thomas R. Burrell observed: "Men of my generation, we are walking into the sunset of a day that is past." For him, the long walk ended on May 23, 1953; he died at his Fall River residence at the age of ninety-one.

He left a legacy of both family and history, the latter of which he documented in compelling prose; clearly, he wrote as he spoke. Despite the fact that he once stated, "Yesterday is gone, tomorrow never was, today is today," he nevertheless had the foresight to document vivid accounts of his collective yesterdays; all are preserved in the collections of the FRHS.

EDITORS' NOTE

On the evening of February 17, 1936, Thomas Richmond Burrell presented his paper, "Main Street in the Eighteen Seventies and Eighties," to the members of the Fall River Historical Society in the parish hall of the First Congregational Church. His presentation, based on his vivid recollections "of those persons who carried on business on Main Street and the central section of the city," was delivered in his amiable, chatty style, to the delight of all those present.

Three years earlier, on May 22, 1933, he had presented his paper, "A Businessman's Reminiscences of Fifty Years," in which he detailed his recollections "of men ... with whom [he] came into contact at the beginning " of his lengthy business career; some of those individuals were also mentioned in his "Main Street" paper.

Although the 1936 paper was not, apparently, conceived as a sequel to the 1933 work, they have been selected by the editors for presentation in this volume due their highly complementary text. Due to the narrative and historical nature of the content, it was decided to publish these two papers in opposite order from which they were originally delivered as lectures.

Contained in this volume are expanded versions of Burrell's original manuscripts, which are housed in the Charlton Library of Fall River History at the Fall River Historical Society. The formats of these manuscripts have been slightly edited for punctuation and readability, with italicized information in square brackets added for the purposes of clarification and context.

Illustrations pertinent to the text have been selected from the collection of photographs and ephemera maintained by the Fall River Historical Society, as well those held in private collections.

In order to preserve the integrity of the original manuscripts, and in an attempt to retain the voice of the author, the phraseology and opinions conveyed in the text remain that of the writer, and do not reflect the views of the Fall River Historical Society.

MAIN STREET IN THE
EIGHTEEN SEVENTIES AND EIGHTIES

At the time that I agreed to write this paper I had the thought that it would be difficult to recall memories which would be of sufficient interest to warrant its writing at all. But, when I opened the gates to the small stream of thought which I anticipated, I found that I was overwhelmed with a flood of memories and that I must be content with grasping one here and there as they whirled through my mind. These are recorded here and are given to you for what they may be worth and with a hope that they may prove interesting.

I have many doubts as to how my friends here may characterize this address at its conclusion. I know it will not be classed as an accurate historical paper, as a literary gem, or as an oratorical treat; I am convinced that it is none of these.

However, from out of the distant past there have come to my mind those persons who carried on business on Main Street and the central section of the city of Fall River, Massachusetts, in the 1870s and early 1880s of the last century. To specify a date when a particular party occupied a particular store would be of little interest to my [readers], and I have written of men and women who were prominent at different times during the period mentioned. Peculiar characters, yes, as we have peculiar characters today, but with the much smaller population these characters were better known and were known by more people than they would have been if living in the present generation.

First, a picture of Main Street in the 1870s: The roadway was an ordinary dirt road, sometimes deeply rutted, with no paving and no macadam. The sidewalk was flat stone slabs, and later came what we called tar sidewalks, which were melted tar and fine gravel mixed, rolled, and

2. View of the east side of North Main Street looking south from Bedford Street, 1870s. "The roadway was an ordinary dirt road, sometimes deeply rutted."

surfaced with a composition of tar and fine sand that was rolled down by hand-rollers similar to those used in rolling lawns.

Now starting at the corner where Smith's Drug Store is located [*105 North Main Street, at the time this paper was written*] was the Massasoit National Bank, of which Leander Borden (1807-1894), father of Eric Warren Borden (1848-1921), was cashier. Eric was the clerk, and these two, with a messenger-boy, comprised the staff of the institution.

M.T. Bennett, [*Messadore Toscan Bennett (1815-1890)*] a coal dealer,

3. View of South Main Street looking south from Pocasset and Pleasant Streets, early 1870s.

and Clinton Van Santvoort Remington (1839-1920), cotton and cloth broker, occupied a large double office on the ground floor. Afterward Samuel R[*obinson*] Buffington & Company occupied one office.

At one time, the Western Union Telegraph Office was located in this building. William P. Potter (1833-1906) was the manager and he had an extra little finger on his right hand. This was very conspicuous when he was engaged in sending and receiving messages and, if a boy had a visitor from the country, it was a great stunt to take him to the telegraph office and show him Mr. Potter's extra digit.

Johnnie [*John H.*] Boone (1829-1921), the merchant tailor, was in this block, and it is a peculiar fact that nearly all of these merchants were called

4. Rolling macadam paving on Bedford Street.

by some such familiar name even by the children, not to their faces of course, but it did not seem disrespectful to so refer to them and it was the common practice.

Elisha Fuller (1824-1918) conducted a large grocery store in this building, and here the operation of such a store might be described, showing the contrast with present day merchandising. Goods were not designated by trade names. There was only one kind of cracker, the hard double cracker which was always kept in a barrel and sold by the pound. Sugar was either white or brown, and also kept in barrels provided with a scoop to put it into the scales. By the way, everything from cod-fish to

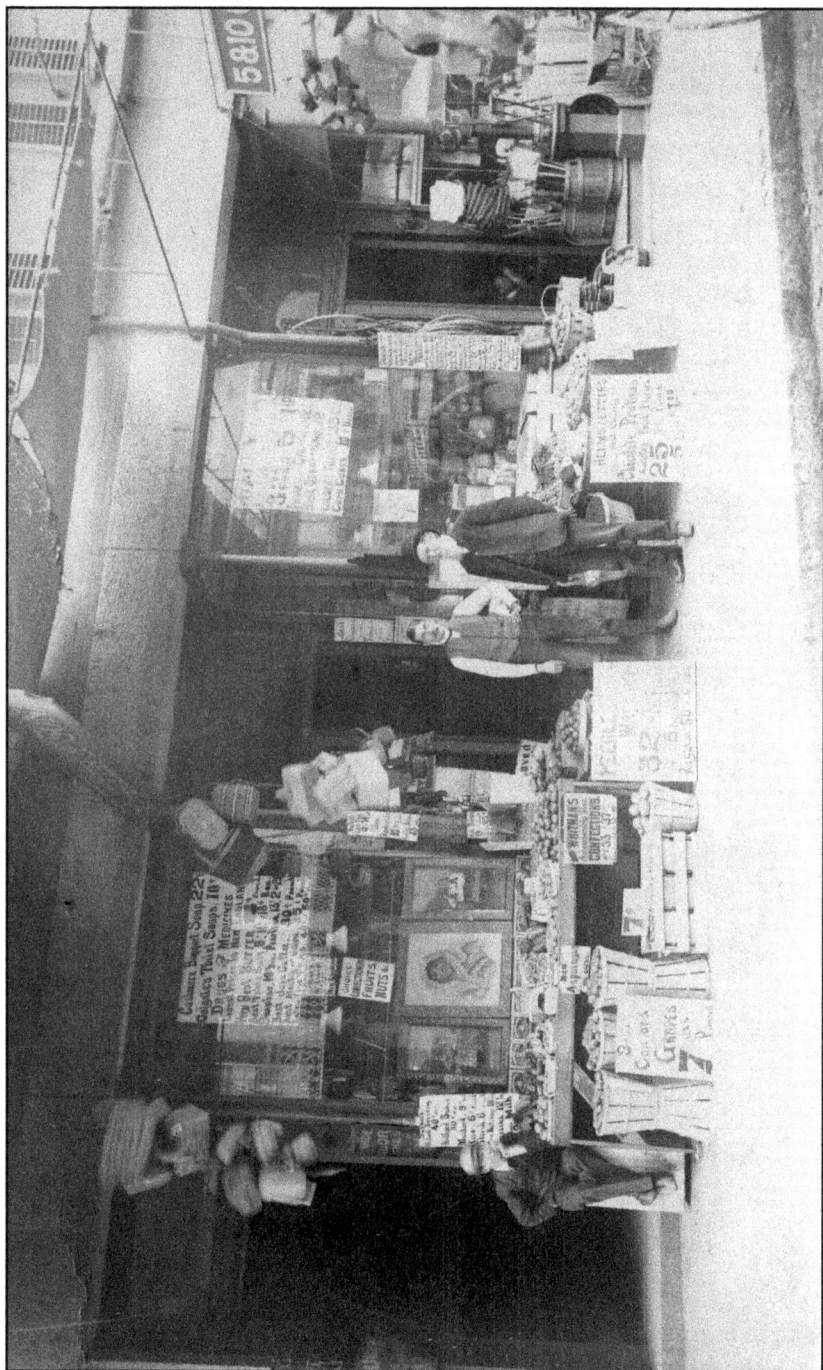

5. Storefront of Elijah Fuller & Son, grocers, 24 North Main Street, 1888. Standing in the doorway are, at the left, Thomas Waning Fuller (1849-1933) with his father, Elisha Fuller (1824-1918), beside him. The boy seated at the far left remains unidentified. .

6. Interior view of Elijah Fuller & Son, grocers, 24 North Main Street, 1887-1888.

7. An unidentified clerk at Elijah Fuller & Son, grocers, 24 North Main Street, 1887-1888.

sugar was weighed on the same scales; sometimes the storekeeper would blow the dust or the meal or flour out of the scales, but not often, and I never remember seeing one wiped or washed. Molasses was bought by the quart, either New Orleans Molasses, light, or Porto Rico Molasses, dark. Later on came granulated sugar, a luxury, and milk crackers, also a great luxury.

Soap came in long bars, either yellow or white, and the housewives cut it into convenient shapes at home. French Laundry Soap was the first soap to be sold in smaller bars and to be wrapped in separate papers with printed labels; this soap was used both for laundry and toilet purposes. [*"Soapine," a French Laundry Soap made by Kendall Manufacturing Company, Providence, Rhode Island, was widely available in Fall River during the third quarter of the nineteenth century. This is evidenced by numerous extant trade cards for the product, bearing the imprint of various Fall River retail establishments.*]

Paper bags were not used or even heard of at that time. All goods were laid on flat paper and then made up into packages by the salesmen. Very few book accounts were kept in the store. The customer was supplied with a store- or pass-book and the charges were entered at the time of purchase and handed back to the customer; at the end of the month the book was presented. The storekeeper footed it up and settlement was made on the amount arrived at. Cash registers were not known, but many of the stores had alarm bells on the money drawer, which rang sharply whenever the drawer was opened.

On the second and third floors was the Mount Hope House, [*a hotel in operation from 1870 to 1876*] conducted by Solomon "Sol" Hooper (1822-1877), a half-brother of Dr. Foster Hooper (1805-1877), and father of Charlie [*Charles Edward*] Hooper (1848-1922) of Pilgrim Band fame. [*A talented musician, Hooper served in various managerial and directorial capacities with: Third Regiment Band, 1880 – circa 1884; Hooper's Band and Orchestra, 1885 – circa 1886; and Hooper's Pilgrim Band, 1887 – circa 1897. The Pilgrim Band was highly successful, and was a favorite among members of Fall River's elite families.*]

"Sol" Hooper was a tall, red-haired, red-whiskered man of limited capital, and it was said that he would wait to ascertain how many were to dine at his table, and would buy as little as a quarter of a pound of butter or a pint of milk in order to be sure and have enough, but not to carry a surplus stock.

8. "French Laundry Soap was the first soap to be sold in smaller bars." Trade card for Soapine, manufactured by Kendall Mfg. Co., Providence, Rhode Island.

9. Reverse of Soapine trade card. Its manufacturer claimed: "Once Tried! Always Used!"

10. Mount Hope House, 57 and 63 North Main Street, depicted at left, was in operation from 1870-1876.

The Five Cents Savings Bank occupied one store numbered 55 North Main Street at one time, and the Fall River Savings Bank occupied the corner. When the Fall River Savings Bank built their building [*on North Main Street, in 1869*], the Five Cents moved into the vacated premises on the corner. Two wide stone steps ran the whole front of the building as well as in front of the Fall River National Bank on the opposite corner. This building [*called the Durfee Block*] was owned by Dr. Nathan Durfee (1799-1876) and he visited it almost daily.

On the Bank Street side of this building were apartments, or tenements, as we called them, occupied by such well-known families as: David Sewall Brigham (1823-1893) [*and his son,*] George Sewall Brigham (1858-1927); William A. Anthony (1840-1891); Captain Charles Dyer Copeland (1828-1912); and Israel Gardner (1818-1877), father of Israel P[*eckham*] Gardner (1848-1932) of the Fall River Savings Bank. My own family lived in the first apartment east from Main Street. On Bank Street lived: Herbert A. Skinner (1828-1907); Dr. Duncan [*Rev. Dr. John Duncan (1820-1884)*] of the Second Baptist Church; Mrs. Hannah Valentine Durfee (1828-1907) [*formerly Mrs. Thomas Lewis Robinson*]; Dr. Jerome Dwelly (1823-1913); Vernon Thurston (1815-1885); Dr. Isaac Smith Jr. (1841-1882); Dr. James W[*ardle*] Hartley (1827-1897); Fredrick Walter Macomber (1825-1886), and others of like standing in the community.

Understand, there was no city water at that time; city water was installed about 1874. [*Burrell's statement is substantiated in a brief history of the Water Works in Fall River, included in the* Report of the Watuppa Water Board to the City Council of Fall River, *published in 1875: "The engine was started on the 5th of January, 1874; and on the 8th the water was in the mains as far as Main Street. On May 8, 1874, about twelve miles of cast iron pipe had been laid, and 100 service connections had been attached."*]

We had a pump in the sink, but the water was unfit for drinking purposes, and all of the boys, before starting for school in the morning, made a trip to a well and drew one or two pails of water for their mothers to use for cooking and drinking. The use of this well was granted as a neighborly courtesy by the owner, whose name I do not recall.

Very few houses had bath tubs because there was no running water. It was customary to take an ordinary wash tub into the kitchen Saturday night, heat a kettle of water and use it in the tub. With a large family, when the members used the kitchen in rotation, this was rather a prolonged ceremony. Bear in mind, I am not speaking of cheap apartments but of the homes of the well-to-do.

11. Dr. Nathan Durfee. A prominent Fall River businessman, he visited his business block "almost daily."

12. Dr. Durfee's Block, corner North Main and Central Streets, depicted during the conflagration on March 2, 1893. The damage from the fire was $8,420, a considerable sum at the time.

Benny [*Benjamin*] Shove (1810-1894), a quaint little Quaker, had a small carpenter shop at the corner of Rock and Bank Streets where the Central Congregational Church Parish House is now located.

You see how easy it is for me to wander from Main Street.

On the south-east corner [*of Bank Street*], of course, was the old Fall River National Bank. A small store in the bank building south of the banking rooms was occupied by Martin Van Buren Benson (1835-1907), who kept a notion [*"fancy goods"*] store, and it certainly was filled with notions. Small articles from pins and needles to hair nets and bustles, all jumbled together, and it seemed to me that the clerks were forever engaged in straightening out the stock but never wholly succeeding in doing so. Those clerks, Miss Josie [*Josephine Brown*] Mason (1851-1921), and Miss Hattie [*Harriet F.*] Huntsman (1844-1915), each pretty of face, with a refined aristocratic bearing, perfect sales people but withal maintaining a quiet dignity that carried the mark of the well-bred, well-reared lady.

13. Fall River National Bank, southeast corner of North Main and Bank Streets, 1890.

14. Trade card for Mount Hope Market, 39 North Main Street, 1880s. Advertising trade cards were popular collectibles during the late-nineteenth century.

Next was James Davis (1814-1888), Mount Hope Market, afterwards known as Davis and Fish, [*John M. Davis (1844-1912) and Asa F. Fish (1841-1921)*]; this market was noted for the high character of its goods and was a display center for market goods. With all the improvements in merchandising, I never have seen a market so perfect in all its appointments as this one. The market opened before daylight and the stock for the day was prepared. At an early hour, three covered butcher carts stood in front and were loaded preparatory to starting on different routes, calling at the doors of the housewives supplying them with meat, butter, lard, and so forth, for the day. The presiding geniuses of these carts were Billy [*William H.*] Sherman (1831-1912), Ferdinand Wilmarth Sherman (1835-1923), and Ferdinand Wilmarth (1818-1903), all members of prominent families and artists in the cutting and preparing of meats for their trade.

Next was John Nowell (1801-1842), father of John Proudfet Nowell (1828-1908), and grandfather of John Proudfet Nowell Jr. (1875-1963). He was a tinsmith. Don't think for a moment that these men carried any outward sign of their business; they dressed like gentlemen at all times. Mr. Nowell sat in front of his store tilted back in a chair, it seemed to me, all the time. If you wanted a tinker's job done in the summer-time, Mr. Nowell would not do it because it was too hot to start a fire in his tinker's stove, and would convince you of the wisdom of this, make you like it, and you would gladly wait for a cooler day to have your work done. However, Mr. Nowell was a substantial citizen and accumulated his full share of this world's goods.

Next south was George W. Nowell (1825-1891), the candy man ["*confectioner and baker*"]. I don't know his age at the time but he seemed very old to us, which he wasn't. His candy was mostly in sticks all made on the premises and displayed in small, glass jars with metal tops. A penny a stick; my mouth waters now as I think of that display. A penny in those days meant nothing but the equivalent of a stick of George Nowell's molasses candy. He was a kindly man with a quiet smile which warmed the hearts of the children and made them feel that he was conferring a favor in exchanging a stick of his candy for their pennies. He, too, prospered and accumulated a competency.

James Barney Chace (1826-1893) and Jonathan Chace (1821-1891) owned the next lot, and William Read Bush (1832-1923) and my father, John Bates Burrell (1825-1883) occupied the ground floor [*Bush at 27½ North Main Street, and Burrell at 27 North Main Street*]. Mr. Bush owned the building and these Chaces would not give him a lease extending over a year. Mr. Bush was haunted with the fear that his lease would not be renewed and he would lose his building, and this finally happened. Mr. Bush was a coppersmith and plumber, and my father, as you know, was a harness-maker.

Next in the Wilbur House hotel building was Wilbur, Cone & Company, [*Leander Davenport Wilbur (1831-1894); Oscar J. Cone (1829-1892); and Benjamin F. Simmons (1826-1896), "merchant tailors"*]. In connection with the ready-made department, Mr. Simmons conducted a custom tailoring department assisted by his nephew, George Frank Allen (1851-1903) [*always called G. Frank Allen*]. Nearly everyone at this time wore paper collars; they came a dozen in a box, price fifteen cents. I recall that Elmwood Collars were rated as the best and were the first article sold by name. [*Widely popular, Elmwood Collars were patented on September 12, 1871, and manufactured by the Narragansett Collar Company, Boston, Massachusetts.*]

Next was Kingsley Express Office. Frank [*Francis D.*] Blake (1820-1896) was the head clerk, and Caleb C. Potter (1846-1912) and John Burns were employed there. Two stages made the Express Office their terminal [*Earle & Prew Express Company, Providence, Rhode Island, and Hatch & Company, Express, New Bedford, Massachusetts*]. One made daily trips

15. Storefront of John B. Burrell, harness and trunk maker, 50 Pocasset Street, 1876. Pictured are John B. Burrell (second from left), and his employees, John Cardin (second from right), and Diendonne Belhumeur (at right). John B. Burrell was the father of the author.

16. View of the east side of North Main Street, showing the Wilbur House, 25-33 North Main Street, circa 1902.

through Little Compton, Rhode Island, to Newport, Rhode Island, and one through the Head of Westport, Massachusetts, to New Bedford. These stages were the exact replicas of the pictures which you have seen of Western stages; in lieu of springs, they were supported by wide leather braces at least a foot wide, so that the body swayed from one side to the other, and fore and aft like a steamboat. The front and back seats faced each other, and between was a swinging seat with a single wide leather strap to support the passengers' backs. The through-fare either to Newport or New Bedford was one dollar. Changes of horses were made at Tiverton and Little Compton, Rhode Island, and Westport.

Darius Wilbur (1816-1883), called "King," was proprietor of the Wilbur House Hotel. He was by profession a cook and in earlier days was chef at the noted West Island Club off Sakonnet Point, Rhode Island. [*Founded in 1865, as "an association for angling and shooting purposes," the West Island Club boasted an elite membership comprising some of the wealthiest and most influential businessmen and politicians in the United States. Membership was limited to thirty men, who paid a subscription fee of $1,000. The organization disbanded in 1907.*]

17. Darius "King" Wilbur. "He was a plump little man of clean-cut features and wore his hair curled under at the back of the neck."

Wilbur owned the house on Purchase Street now [*in 1936*] occupied by Dr. Edward Herbert (1875-1944) and his family resided there and not at the hotel. He was a plump little man of clean-cut features and wore his hair curled under at the back of the neck; I wonder if anybody ever wears the hair in that style in these days. Mr. Wilbur wore blue clothes, a short sack coat, and with his ample waistline made a conspicuous figure on the street. His watch chain was hung with three, $5, $10, and $20 gold pieces. He kept no bank account, all of his funds being carried in his clothes. I have many times presented him with drafts for liquors and he would call me in the back room, out of sight, and drawing rolls of bills from his several pockets pay at once, regardless of whether the draft was payable on demand, or thirty or sixty days hence. And I might note that he bought the finest of liquors from the same firms that the best druggists patronized.

On the opposite corner of Granite Street, then Court Street, was Pollard's Drug Store [*Darius W. Pollard (1830-1894), "apothecary"*], afterwards Anthony & Dunbar [*Edward S. Anthony (1845-1900) & Bradford Dunbar (1843-1896), "druggists"*], then Anthony's [*Edward S. Anthony, druggist*], then Hicks' [*Dr. Charles A. Hicks (1858-1949), business conducted as "Dr. Charles A. Hicks' Anthony's Pharmacy"*].

Next was Shove & Fisher [*"Gent's Furnishing Goods"*], Abe [*Abram Francis*] Shove (1845-1913) and Charlie [*Charles Edward*] Fisher (1846-1914); Fred [*Frederick O.*] Dodge (1855-1934) and Warren Sisson Barker (1857-1930) were clerks in this store. They reported at seven o'clock in the morning and either Mr. Shove or Mr. Fisher would be there. During the night all of the

18. Charles Edward Fisher.

19. Shove & Fisher, hats, caps, and furnishing goods, 11 North Main Street, 1876. Two of the men in the photograph are likely Charles E. Fisher and Abram F. Shove. This popular Fall River establishment was patronized by many of the city's leading families.

exposed goods were covered with long strips of white cloth; these were taken out on the sidewalk each morning, and with a clerk on one end and one of the proprietors on the other, were shaken in the breeze and then carefully folded to await the coming of another night.

Next was Isaiah P. Pope (1818-1882); it would take a better descriptive writer than myself to do justice to this outfit. This was the paper and periodical store [*"periodical depot, fruit, &c."*]. A long counter ran the length of the store with a brass rail in front to keep the papers and magazines in place.

Mr. Pope was a thin, spare old man, stooped, and seemed very old. For clerks, he had three men as old, or older, than he was. One, Mr. [*Edmund H.*] Peirce (1831-1884) wore a thin overcoat summer and winter, with the collar turned up and only the top button fastened. He had the most soul-devastating cough I have ever heard and always seemed to be on the verge of giving the battle up and calling it a day. Another man was a little fellow named Arnold, who had only one eye, and if he wasn't ninety years old he looked it. The third was Isaac Maxon Rider (1831-1896). These men were all judges of good literature and when not busy with customers were always reading. All one had to do was to start an argument and these three would join in and agree neither with you nor with each other.

Next was Westgate's hardware store, on the Bedford Street corner, [*owned by*] Jim Westgate, as everyone called him, [*James F. Westgate (1843-1913)*]. The door was diagonally across the corner and Mr. Westgate sat about six feet inside in a big chair and watched the passers-by, meanwhile keeping an eye on his clerks and customers. He was a finely dressed man of aristocratic bearing, always dressing with extreme care, a long fine gold watch chain around his neck and hanging over his ample stomach.

On the opposite side of Bedford Street where the Citizens Savings Bank building now stands [*in 1936*], was a low wooden building occupied at one time by the Western Union Telegraph Company.

On the Bedford Street side, John Davol Jr. (1822-1904) kept a clothing store, [*"hats, caps, gents' furnishing goods, and periodicals"*]. He was a Civil War Veteran and when the G.A.R. [*Grand Army of the Republic, Richard Borden Encampment, Post 46*] paraded on Memorial Day, John and Sol [*Solomon W.*] Wilbur (1845-1916), after getting properly liquidated, would head the line with their drums, and maybe they couldn't drum. After the parade they would stand on the corner, and keep drumming until darkness settled down or the source of their inspiration lost its fervor. [*John Davol Jr., served as Private, Company C., 3rd Massachusetts Infantry,*]

20. James F. Westgate & Co., hardware and cutlery, 1 North Main Street, corner Bedford, circa 1872. The proprietor was "a finely-dressed man of aristocratic bearing."

and as Private, Company F., 58th Massachusetts Infantry; and Solomon W. Wilbur, served as Private, Unattached 5th & 21st Massachusetts Infantry.]

Over the clothing store was the barber shop of Julius Caesar Mershardo, a handsome Italian, with the most luxuriant beard I have ever seen. [*He was probably referring to Horatio Moncada "hairdresser, 3 North Main Street," circa 1866-1873. According to the U.S. Civil War Draft Registration Records, 1863-1865, Horatio was born in Italy circa 1828. He is last listed in* The Fall River Directory *in 1873. The moniker "Julius Caesar" was possibly in reference to his Italian heritage.*]

Next south on Main Street was another two story wooden building, the second floor being occupied by a photographer named Alfred [*Ellis*]

21. Alfred Ellis Hill, "an original character and an original advertiser."

Hill (1835-1909), an original character and an original advertiser. He held reception nights to which the people generally were invited. To attract the populace, he established a museum and featured, among other things: hens with iridescent plumage, which he prepared by treating their feathers with chemicals used in his profession; a mermaid constructed of a monkey's head attached to a fish's body; and dancing turkeys, two beautiful birds in a box cage with a barred front. These two birds were continually lifting first one foot and then the other in a weird unnatural dance movement. It was afterwards discovered that the floor of the cage was made of zinc under which was concealed a lighted kerosene lamp which kept the floor just hot enough to keep the turkeys moving their feet.

22. The Great American Photograph Company, South Main Street, corner of Bedford, circa 1870. Alfred E. Hill "established a museum and featured, among other things, hens with iridescent plumage, which he prepared by treating their feathers with chemicals used in his profession...."

23. Novelty cabinet card depicting City Hall, before and after the 1886 fire.

Next was the old City Hall before the rebuilding; on the north side of the Main Street entrance was the Pocasset National Bank, and on the south side the National Union Bank. [*The Fall River City Hall was constructed of native granite as the Town Hall and Market Building in 1845. Fall River's growth necessitated the remodeling and enlarging of the structure between 1872 and 1873, when a mansard roof and clock tower were added. The interior of the structure was also rearranged to accommodate the greatly increasing work of the city departments. The building was gutted by fire on March 19, 1886, and was rebuilt along the same lines at a cost of $300,000; there were few changes to the exterior. The building was demolished in November of 1962 to make way for the construction of Interstate 195.*]

The street floor was occupied by meat stalls, on each side of the wide passageway extending from the front to the back of the building. These stalls were narrow divisions with racks on each side with hooks upon which the beef and mutton were suspended. Fresh vegetables were not displayed, only potatoes, beets, turnips and non-perishable goods. This floor was not heated, and the cold blasts of winter had free scope from east to west so that artificial refrigeration was not necessary. Some of the prominent citizens presided over these establishments: Julian T. Pember (1830-1888), "provisions"; Edward P[*urington*] Buffinton (1817-1871), "provisions"; David M. Anthony (1835-1915), "provisions"; Henry Bagshaw & Company, [*brothers, Henry Bagshaw (1830-1878), Bartholomew Bagshaw (1832-1887), and Benjamin Bagshaw (1840-1880), "butchers"*], and men of that type.

A very fleshy man named [*James*] Boomer (1808-1876) had a fish market at the Second Street end in the basement and would dress your fish while you waited, and then lifting a trap door would souse the fish in the stream under City Hall which was thick with the filth from the Troy Cotton & Woolen Manufactory and points beyond. This did not seem so bad to me, but when I mentioned it to my mother [*Mrs. John B. Burrell, née Elizabeth Fales Richmond (1828-1919)*] one day, I was given strict orders to buy no more fish of Mr. Boomer. [*There were surely additional reasons why Mrs. Burrell refused to purchase fish rinsed in the waters of the Quequechan. Not only was the river contaminated by industrial waste, but it was also the recipient of human waste; the public privies were situated on its banks, just east of City Hall and the fishmonger's trap door.*]

There was no delivery system at that time, but Jake [*Jacob*] Sampson (c.1815-1890), more familiarly known as "Dirty Jake," stood at the back door with a wheelbarrow and would deliver your order anywhere in the city for twenty-five cents. [*More often than not, Jacob Sampson was among the city's unemployed, living at the Almshouse; in the* United States Federal

24. View of the Quequechan River, a "victim of industrial growth," looking northwest.

Census – 1880 Schedules of Defective, Dependent, and Delinquent Classes, *under the heading "Paupers and Indigent Inhabitants in Institutions, Poor-Houses or Asylums, or Boarded at Public Expense in Private Houses," he was described as "not able bodied," and "habitually intemperate."*]

You saw no delivery-wagons in the streets, just private carriages of prominent citizens and doctors, and a few hacks and so-called local express-wagons for hire. If you bought a stove, for instance, fifty cents was added to the price to pay for delivery by one of the local expresses.

At the southeast corner of City Hall next to the curbing was the town pump and watering trough; the trough was cut from a solid piece of granite. Drivers stopped their horses here to drink, and when the water became low some driver would refill it by manipulating the tall pump standing at the end. The trough is still in existence [*and, at the time of Burrell's lecture, was*] at the upper farm of Mark [*Marcus Ellsworth*] Wordell (1863-1944) on the Main Road [*North Main Street*] near the Assonet line. He purchased it for $5.00, placed it on his land, and piping a spring above connected the trough, chained a dipper to it, and he delights in supplying callers with a cooling drink and reciting its history. [*The trough passed to Marcus's son,*

Norman Barnaby Wordell (1898-1972) and his wife, née Thelma May Allen (1897-1993), and thus by descent to their daughter, Virginia Mae Wordell (1923-2006), who donated it to the Fall River Historical Society when the farm was sold to a developer in the 1990s. It is now situated on the north lawn at the museum.]

In the building which we know as the Hawkins Building in the corner store at Pleasant and Second Streets, Elihu Andrews (1823-1905) and his brother [*Reuben Hall Andrews (1814-1906)*] conducted a grocery store [*E. & R. H. Andrews*], which was the headquarters for farmers and others from the country, who came into the city to sell their produce and make their purchases to take back home.

As an example of the fact that there is nothing really new in this world, this store was the early quick lunch establishment. There was always an open barrel of crackers and plenty of cheese, with cans of milk standing on the floor. A few glasses which were washed occasionally, if business was not too brisk. You understand everyone helped themselves and paid for what they ate, keeping their own record.

25. Interior of Whitehead's Market, 102 South Main Street.

On the counters were various kinds of pies which were kept under circular, wire fly-screens, and when one of these was lifted and inadvertently left off for a few minutes, it was a master mind that could tell the difference between a mince and a current pie. Later on, local business men found it very convenient to grab a lunch at Andrews' when the wife was attending the Ladies' Sewing Circle or the Good Templars.

There was no fire alarm system at this time, and at the Central Engine House, located at the corner of Court Square, now Granite Street, and what is now Purchase Street, the Metacomet and King Philip engines [*Steam Fire Engine, Metacomet, No. 3, and Steam Fire Engine, King Philip, No. 2*] were housed. In a small tower atop of the Court House, in the same building, a bell was installed. Whenever a fire was located people ran through the streets crying, "Fire," and the first citizen reaching the engine house would grasp the bell rope and ring the bell with might and main. Joe [*Joseph*] Curry (born 1792) and Clark Whipple (1814-1872) drove the sprinkling carts on the streets in the center of the city, and were also the drivers of the engines using the same horses. The minute they heard the bell, they would climb down from the high seats on the water carts, unhitch the horses, and with the whiffletrees clattering along the ground, proceed to the engine house, and attaching the same whiffletrees to the engines, come forth with more excitement and noise than the whole present department makes when called out. [*A whiffletree is a pivoted, swinging bar, to which the traces of a harness are fastened and by which a vehicle is drawn.*] But, of course, they had an army of small boys to assist them in increasing the din and confusion.

In this same building, back of the engine room, was the cell room of the Central Police Station. On the Granite Street side, in the summertime, the outside door of the cell room would be opened, exposing an iron-barred door, and the screaming and cursing of the drunks could be heard on the street.

Next west were the city stables, and the Superintendent of Streets office was a little wooden building on the opposite side. Fred [*Frederick*] J. McLane (1860-1945) of the Fall River Board of Assessors was clerk in this office.

There were four hand-engines. The Cataract [*Engine Company No. 3*] at what was later the G.A.R Hall [*at 116 Rock Street*], the Cascade [*Engine Company, No. 1*] on South Main Street; the Ocean [*Fire Company No. 5*] on Pearl Street, and the Torrent [*Company No. 6*] on North Main Street.

A few men would start these from the houses, and, as they proceeded, staid citizens and small boys would grasp the ropes until a complete

26. Fire department horses on the Third Street bridge, 1889.

force was gathered, and when the fire was reached and the suction-hose connected with the water in the nearest well, the pumper was manned, and the cry, "Pump her up," was heard, and we boys, sandwiched in between grown men, would be pulled two feet from the ground as the pump arms were elevated on the up-sweep. I would hate to have to account for all the falsehoods that were told about the speed with which the fire was reached, how quick the water came through the pumps, and how high a stream was forced.

On Bedford Street, of course, was Allen, Slade & Company [*Howard Bowen Allen (1812-1889); George W. Slade (1826-1912); Edward Bennett Lake (1835-1913); and Benjamin Slade Chase Gifford (1835-1941)*], and Pettey & Lawton [*Asa Pettey Jr. (1820-1893) and Joseph H. Lawton (1826-1898)*], wholesale grocers.

At the corner of Bedford and Purchase Streets, where George Nightingale Durfee's building is located, Mason Fisher & Co. [*Mason Fisher (1819-1903) and George A. Borden (1822-1895)*] had their main bake shop. [*The Durfee Building, owned by George N. Durfee Jr. (1867-1948), had addresses at 60 Bedford Street and 70 Purchase Street; the structure was demolished.*]

In the morning, five or six bake carts, all enclosed, were parked on Bedford Street and the drivers were busy filling the racks inside with pies and cakes; most of the housewives made their own bread, it being considered a sign of financial weakness not to have a barrel of flour in the house at all times. Underneath the carts were little bells attached to springs and as they moved through the streets these little bells gave forth a tinkling sound giving notice of their approach, and it was a common sight to see a woman standing at the front door of her home, pie plate in hand, waiting for the baker's cart as it came along the street. Yeast cakes came long after this and Mason Fisher & Co. sold yeast by the pint. You brought your own pitcher and delivered your own yeast.

Edwin F. Manchester (1842-1900) had a harness-making shop next to Mason Fisher & Co.'s bake shop, and Deacon Charles Coburn (1819-1891), also a harness-maker, was located opposite the City Hall in Market Square.

27. View looking east up Granite Street from North Main Street, circa 1910. The Central Police Station and the entrance to the jail are depicted in the last building on the right.

28. Bakery delivery carts assembled in front of Mason Fisher & Co. Steam Bakery, 37 Bedford Street, circa 1859. "They did a very large business."

Mason Fisher & Co. built the Fall River Opera House on Court Street, now Purchase Street, and they did a very large business, the so-called "legitimate plays" being produced before the erection of the Academy of Music. [*The Fall River Opera House possessed a scandalous reputation; it was located on Court Square, a block from the Richardson House hotel, and right across the street from the Central Police Station. Advertised as "excellently ventilated, lighted and heated," the auditorium had a seating capacity of 1,000. But the claim that legitimate theatre was performed there was apparently not the case for very long, and the Opera House quickly became quite controversial. Little has survived as to what went on inside, but the theatre, a victim of public outcry that was referred to as a "hell hole," had a very short-lived existence.*]

29. Fall River Opera House, Court Square, 1880. The so-called "legitimate plays" were produced here "before the erection of the Academy of Music."

Opposite where the Post Office stands, Hathaway & Deane [*Alonzo Hathaway (born 1834) and John Milton Deane (1840-1914), grocers*] had a large store, and "Peanut Hathaway" [*Joseph R. Hathaway (1832-1904), "coffee manufacturer"*] roasted peanuts in the adjoining building on Second Street. Next south on Second Street, Asa Eames (1886-1909) had a carriage manufactory.

On the Bedford Street side where the Post Office was located, east of Hathaway and Deane, were two one-story blacksmith shops, one, W. & J.M. Osborn [*Weaver Osborn (1815-1894) and James M. Osborn*], and the other, N. Pearce & Son [*Nathaniel A. Pearce (1841-1923) and Nathaniel Pearce*

(1809-1878)]. Charles P. Newell (born 1837) conducted [*an upholstery and*] furniture business, located between the Pocasset National Bank and the National Union Bank, after they left the City Hall when it was to be rebuilt.

Lincoln & Kelley, jewelers, occupied the corner of Main and Market Streets [*George W. Lincoln (1834-1907) and Zeno Kelley (1823-1868), "watchmakers and jewelers"*].

Before Almy & Milne [*Thomas Almy (1819-1882) and John Cruikshank Milne (1823-1918), "job printers and publishers"*] bought the property at the corner of Pleasant and Second Streets, the *Fall River News* was published from the second floor of this building, and now I am going back to the Civil War period of the 1860s. [*Established in 1845, the* Fall River News *was published by Thomas Almy & John C. Milne, for weekly circulation on Thursday mornings. Described as "An Independent Family Journal," the newspaper continued under that name for over fifteen years; by 1861, two separate periodicals were produced through this publisher:* Fall River Daily News *and* Fall River Weekly News.]

My brother, John Thaxter Burrell (1857-1904), has often told me that when news of a big battle came, he, with other boys of his age, seven or eight years, sold Extras and were often called from their beds at night by messengers sent out by Franklin Lawton Almy (1833-1912) for this work. Main Street would be solid with men, and Mr. Almy would load the boys with all the papers they could carry and help them through the window; the boys would work their way hand over hand along the awning frames, and then drop into the crowd. My brother said that it seemed to him that they hardly touched the ground before all of the papers were sold – nobody waiting for change – and then he would wiggle his way back to the stairway and repeat the performance. He sold Extras when the news of [*President Abraham*] Lincoln's assassination was received in April, 1865. He was born in April, 1857, so at the end of the war could only have been eight years old. My father has told me how he stood in the crowd and cried when he heard that childish voice in the night crying, "Extras."

All the stores kept open five nights a week until nine o'clock when the bell on the Court House was rung to announce the hour. On Thursday nights, stores were closed at seven o'clock to allow proprietors and clerks to attend prayer meetings, which were held at all the churches downtown. A few of the stores still were lighted by kerosene lamps, the others by gas, generally with T-shaped fixtures, two dim lights to each fixture, with a porcelain shade attached to the ceiling over each light to guard against fire. The show windows were equipped with panes of glass not less than six and sometimes ten lights to a window. Very few plate glass windows existed at that time.

The streets were lighted by street lights topping wooden poles. A few in the center [*of the city*] were equipped with one flickering gas jet, while a few larger number held a tin container filled with kerosene; three wicks enclosed in three prong-like fingers attached to the container and carried the fluid by capillary attraction. Lamplighters equipped with a ladder and a basket of filled lamps went from corner to corner, replacing the exhausted lamps of the night before with the filled ones. On blowy, stormy nights, frequently the wind would blow the lights out almost as fast as they were lighted. [*Kerosene was the predominent method of lighting during this period, but even with the advent of gas lights, and later, electric lighting, fluid lighting use was still considerable. As late as the 1890s, more than half of the street lighting in Fall River, over five hundred lamps, were lit by kerosene. The lighting method did not become fully outmoded until 1916.*]

Mail was delivered to houses, stores, and offices, by postmen who received two cents for each letter delivered, which was their compensation, and from which the name of the "penny post" was derived. This, of course, had nothing to do with postage, which was required, as now. Two one-armed veterans, Darius F. Negus (1841-1911), and Joseph Harrison (1836-1927), were the postmen, and they slid the letters with thumb and finger, handicapped by the fact that they had only one hand to work with. [*Darius F. Negus, Private, Company D, 4th Rhode Island Infantry; and Joseph Harrison, Corporal, Company G, 26th Massachusetts Infantry. The latter was wounded on September 19, 1864, in Winchester, Virginia, during the Third Battle of Winchester, a.k.a. Battle of Opequon, necessitating the amputation of his left arm.*]

Charlie [*Charles M.*] Horton (1841-1903) was at one time a "penny post," and afterwards stamp clerk in the Post Office. Of course, advertising by mail was unheard of at that time and most of the mail was business or personal.

Next south of the City Hall was the Pocasset Block. At the north end, R.S. Gibbs & Company [*Robert Sheffield Gibbs (1816-1885) and George W. Gibbs (1821-1882), "clothing and furnishing goods,"*] carried on a custom tailoring establishment, and at one time the Post Office occupied the south front corner, but later moved to the corner of Rock and Bedford Streets, while the Post Office [*Custom House*] Building, recently demolished [*in 1931*] was being constructed. [*Construction of the Post Office Custom House Building began in 1875, and was not completed until 1880; the building,*]

30. Lamplighter in Fall River circa 1890.

31. Metacomet Bank building, Bedford Street. An ornate cast-iron streetlight stands in the foreground.

however, opened for business in 1876.] Chester Washington Greene (1811-1896) was postmaster, and Walter Frank Shove (1858-1931), clerk. [*The latter was always referred to as W. Frank Shove.*]

Jabez Taber Nye (1823-1882) occupied a part of the basement of the Pocasset Block with an oyster saloon [*the "Pocasset Eating House"*].

The present firm of G.M. Haffards Company [*Albert Timon Borden (1867-1951) and James A. Griffiths (1873-1936), "stocks, bonds, real estate, and insurance,"*] at one time occupied the south corner under the name of Covel, Haffards & Company [*Alphonso Smith Covel (1842-1907), Griffiths Morse Haffards (1845-1906), and Captain James C. Brady (1830-1909), "bankers"*]; the last for many years was city treasurer.

Greene & Son [*Chester Washington Greene (1811-1896) and William Stedman Greene (1841-1924), "auctioneers, real estate, and stock brokers,"*] occupied part of the second floor, and George Salisbury (1832-1897) published the *Weekly Advance* from this building; the first "yellow journal" carrying all the personal gossip of the day, later it became a strong labor organ. [*Published from 1879 to 1888 as a weekly, the newspaper was contemporaneously described in the* American Newspaper Annual: *"The [Weekly] Advance is published every Saturday, is a bright, lively, chatty, and humorous paper, and is a great favorite with the reading public. Though only established in March, 1879, it has already become the most popular and best read paper in the district. It is a family paper, a home paper, and a business man's paper, and has already won a circulation second to none in the city, and a popularity greater than that of every one of its local contemporaries. As an advertising medium it has no equal in the district, reaching every class of readers, and being appreciated by all."*]

Previous to the erection of the Borden Block, the east side of Main Street was lined with small wooden buildings, some of the tenants being: Niels Arnzen (1816-1906), "jewelry &c."; Susan M. Ballard (1818-1885), "fancy goods" [*Mrs. Alvan Sampson Ballard, nèe Susan M. Godfrey*]; Timothy J. Nooning (1840-1924), "millinery and fancy goods"; William A. Anthony (1839-1878) "fruit and confectionery"; and others as well-known.

South of the Borden Block site was the shoe store of Stephen L. French

32. Advertisement for the *Weekly Advance*, 1880.

(1803-1885), father of Enoch Judson French (1851-1936); the family lived over the store for many years.

Henry Strassman (1830-1898) owned the property just south of this and conducted a clothing business there. [*He operated a "dry goods" establishment, at 34 South Main Street, and was a partner in Strassman*

33. View of South Main Street looking north toward City Hall, circa 1874. The first phase of the excavation for the Borden Block foundation can be seen at the immediate right of this image.

& Boas, clothing, at 36 South Main Street, with David S. Boas (1851-1920)].
This was really the first Jewish family that became prominent and certainly
his son, [*Henry K. Strassman (1862-1934)*], and daughter, [*Etta Strassman
(1859-1949) the wife of Maurice K. Burger (circa 1852-1917)*], were the first
Jewish children to graduate from the Fall River High School, being of the
class of which our [*Fall River Historical Society*] President, [*Oliver Snow
Hawes (1860-1938)*] is so proud, 1879.

At the corner of South Main and Borden Streets where Hudner's
Market is now located [*in 1936*], Flint, Grant & Nichols or "Flunt, Grunt,
and Knuckles" sold furniture, stoves, and tin ware: John Dexter Flint (1826-
1907); Rev. Elihu Grant (1820-1897); and Lafayette Nichols (1824-1896). A
long platform ran the length of the front, and ranges and parlor stoves were
on display outside the store at all times during the day. In the morning, a
long line of tin peddlers' carts stood in front; these carts were enclosed and
the sides could be lifted up displaying crockery, earthenware, etc. Hanging
along the sides was tin ware of all kinds—pans, cups, pails and the like;
mops and brooms were attached to the rear, stuck through iron hoops. A
large burlap bag always hung from the back. These carts traveled through
the countryside exchanging the tin ware and other articles for rags, which
were placed in the bags, brought in, sorted and sold.

John D. Flint afterwards built the Flint Exchange [*a commercial block*].
Mr. Nichols opened the store ["*L. Nichols & Company, "house furnishing
goods, furniture, stoves etc.*"] at Pleasant and Third Streets, [*Lafayette
Nichols (1824-1896) and his son, Albert Lafayette Nichols (1849-1924)*] and
Elihu Grant became his bookkeeper. Mr. Grant was a classmate of General
Ulysses Simpson Grant (1822-1885) at West Point Military Academy, and
William Thomas Grant (1876-1972), founder of the W. T. Grant Stores [*a
famous American department store chain founded in Lynn, Massachusetts,
in 1906*] is his grandson. Elihu Grant was an ordained preacher of the
Methodist Episcopal Church. [*A Civil War veteran, Elihu Grant served as
Captain, Company C, Third Massachusetts Infantry.*]

Beyond Borden Street on the east side, Gardner T. Dean (1816-1888)
kept a grocery store at the corner of Rodman Street, and this was looked
upon as the end of business to the south. Mr. Dean lived on Pine Street,
east of Main Street; he was a finely dressed man, a solid citizen, and highly
esteemed.

Bradford Matthew Chaloner Durfee (1843-1872) lived [*on North Main
Street*] where the bank and part of the Fall River Public Library are now
located; south of the residence, a lane [*Borden Avenue*] ran down to the

34. John Dexter Flint. "Few men had the confidence in his own judgment and acted upon it as Mr. Flint did."

35. Trade card for J.D. Flint & Co. (stoves, tinware, house furnishing goods), 1880s.

36. Residence of Mary (Brayton) Durfee Young and her son, Bradford Matthew Chaloner Durfee, 72 North Main Street, 1872.

stables. William Jeff (1843-1912), who Mr. Durfee brought over from England, was the coachman for a number of years. Mr. Durfee imported four Percheron Stallion from Russia together with heavy russet leather harnesses. He had a drag, which was a carriage with side seats that would accommodate six people on each side, with a door and steps at the rear so that the occupants sat high above the wheels, with the owner, and coachman, still higher on the driver's seat. With the four Russian horses, two bays and two grays, it was an impressive sight as they came out of the lane and tooled through Main Street.

37. M. Fisher & Co. Domestic Bakery, 50 North Main Street, corner West Bank Street, circa 1882. Mason Fisher is second from right, with Charlie [Charles] Jones at the far right. Henry Baker is at the far left. The rest of the individuals standing in front of the business remain unidentified. Mason Fisher's son, George Boutwell Fisher, can be seen looking out the second-story window at right.

Mason Fisher & Co. had a baker shop at the corner of West Bank and North Streets; Bilson Page (1810-1876), a carpet [*and "paper hangings'*] store; and John C. Brightman (1845-1910), a cigar [*and tobacco*] store with a large wooden Indian in front, which was taken into the store every night. Steve [*Stephen*] Shove (1820-1888), the [*watchmaker and*] jeweler, Horace Bean (1819-1904), the tailor, up one flight, Jarvis Teal Marble (1828-1902), also upstairs, with his unique sign: "Violins and Oysters." My father, John B. Burrell, and then Chace, Waite & Grouard, the painters [*James B. Chace, Andrew J. Waite (circa 1829-1900), and John E. Grouard (1824-1887)*].

Job Borden French (1806-1894), the "Smoothing Iron," [*was*] so-called because of his careful avoidance of disagreements. [*He was*] tall, stooped-shouldered and silk-hatted, [*and wore a*] Prince Albert coat; he always carried his hands in the sleeves of his coat when he walked the streets. He fitted up a very modern store for the times, but there was little possibility for display because shoes did not come in separate boxes, but were tied in pairs, and packed in deep drawers, arranged in the sides of the store.

Joseph Learned Buffinton (1842-1906), hardware, [*at 18 North Main Street*]; Charles Frank (born 1825) and William Hoar Ashley (1817-1895), clothing; and at the corner of Central Street, Daniel Stillwell (1825-1878), "hardware and cutlery," in a small two-story building.

The Richardson House hotel, occupied the stories above these stores and a long balcony ran the length of the front faced with an iron grating. In political campaigns it was customary for the orators to address the populace from this balcony. [*The Richardson House advertised "one hundred and twenty-five nicely furnished rooms for permanent and transient guests … the largest lodging house in the city."*]

Now, the Granite Block [*a commercial building on "Main between Pocasset and Central" streets*]; it used to be a stunt to name the occupants of the stores without looking at them. This I am not going to try to do, but will from memory speak of a number of them. The block was quite shallow at that time and the stores were narrow when compared with modern establishments.

At the north end was the First National Bank, with the elder John Summerfield Brayton (1826-1904) presiding; Charles A. Bassett (1842-1916) was cashier, and George S. Baker (1850-1875) and Everett M. Cook (1855-1931) were tellers.

Joseph E. Chace (1810-1878) [*and his son, Joseph W. Chace (1831-1881),*] had a drug store near the north end selling mostly herbs. He was a large baby-faced man, and sported a canopy-topped carriage and a pair of Bay

38. Agricultural Warehouse and Richardson House, which boasted "one hundred and twenty-five nicely furnished rooms for permanent and transient guests," located at the corner of North Main and Central Streets.

horses. He was always alone, holding the ribbons and never looking to the right or the left. Next was Dodge & Sears, Boots and Shoes [*John Earl Dodge (1827-1898) and Isaiah Francis Sears (1845-1925)*], afterwards, Mrs. M. A. Mather, Boots and Shoes. [*"Mrs. M. A. Mather" was, in fact, Mrs. Charles M.S. Gerry, née Mary E. Mather (1839-1908); following the death of her brother, George W. Mather (1844-1871), a dealer in "boots and shoes" in Fall River, she operated his former business until circa 1877.*]

At [*12 Granite Block*] was Willard & Mason [*Artemas Willard (1800-1881) and John Mason Jr. (1812-1885) "hardware"*]. "Possum" Willard sat in front of his store in the summertime clad in a linen suit, wet through with perspiration, asleep most of the time. He was dubbed "Possum" because of the feeling that it was safe to watch your step when trading with him. Shattergood Baines in the stories [*by Clarence Budington Kelland (1881-1964)*] in the *American Magazine* is a prototype of "Possum" Willard.

39. Granite Block, Fall River, Massachusetts, early 1890s.

Joseph Abraham Bowen (1832-1914), the coal dealer, habitually went to his office mounted on a chestnut horse, often with his little daughter [*Fanny Corey Bowen (1869-1940)*] in front of him on the saddle. He would dismount and go into his office, paying no more attention to the horse who would wander aimlessly about the street, and, if a load of hay passed, he would follow on grabbing mouthfuls of hay as he proceeded. When Mr. Bowen required the horse's services the whole available populace were kept busy searching for him.

Milne & Mackenzie, [*Alexander T. Milne (1835-1905) and Judson Cary Mackenzie (1852-1930), "boots, shoes, and sewing machines," was at 10 Granite Block and was*] afterwards called Milne & McGraw [*Alexander T. Milne and Frank McGraw (1833-1892), "boots and shoes."*]

H[*endrick*] Gordon Webster (1848-1919), [*"apothecary" at 8 Granite Block,*] afterwards [*occupied by the drug store of*] Benjamin Frank Riddell (1846-1927).

40. Joseph Abraham Bowen. "He would dismount and go into his office, paying no more attention to [*his*] horse who would wander aimlessly about the street, and, if a load of hay passed, [*the horse*] would follow on grabbing mouthfuls of hay as he proceeded."

41. Fanny Corey Bowen. Her father, a "coal dealer, habitually went to his office mounted on a chestnut horse, often with his little daughter in front of him on the saddle."

Billy Bennett's Drug Store [*William Gray Bennett (1832-1900)*] in the center of the block; if a farmer raised a large squash, if a child caught a peculiar bug, or if a woman knit a prize scarf, it was displayed in Bennett's window. [*At the age of twenty-one, Billy Bennett had been employed at the drug and apothecary establishment of John Russell (1813-1853) located at 8 Granite Block. Within two years, Bennett had assumed the business, operating it under his own name at this location for over forty years, thereby becoming an institution of sorts in Fall River. The quaint window displays in his store only enhanced the small-town atmosphere that was so prevalent in the city.*]

Next was Nathan Read & Company, [*Nathan Read (1806-1895), John Read (1810-1895), and Theodore E. Read (1840-1878),*] the hatter ["*hats,*

42. Interior of Bennett's Drug Store, 2 North Main Street, late 1880s. William G. Bennett, proprietor, is behind the counter on the right.

caps, and furs"]; then Rodman & Sargent [*Francis C. Rodman (1819-1873) and Leroy Sargent (1838-1881), "dry goods and woolens"*], afterwards Leroy Sargent [*"dry goods"*], who made a specialty of Jesse Eddy's woolens [*manufactured in Fall River at Wamsutta Woolen Mills; Jesse Eddy (1801-1873) and his son, Thomas Fry Eddy (1827-1886) were proprietors of the firm*].

Next came Philip S. Brown (1802-1877) [*"botanic medicines"*]; Benjamin Earl (1809-1884), [*"books, stationery, &c."*]; Frederick Walter Macomber (1825-1886), [*"jeweler"*], afterwards Aime B[*enjamin*] Bruneau (born 1844); Holt & Henry [*William H. Holt (1824-1908) and James W. Henry, "dry goods"*]; Marvel & Munroe [*John B. Marvel (1803-1890) and Thomas G. Munroe (1846-1928), 'dry goods'*]; and at Liggett's corner, Allen & Hathaway [*Samuel Allen (1820-1896), and William James Hathaway (1838-1902)*], dry goods. [*"Liggett's corner" refers to the location of Liggett-Brady Drug Store, later Liggett's Drug Store, located at 47 South Main Street, at the corner of Pocasset Street, from 1932 to 1961.*]

On the opposite side of Pocasset Street was Elias Augustus Tuttle (1843-1907), the auctioneer, who held an auction every Saturday in the basement, mounted on a box, coat and vest off, with a voice that carried an unlimited distance; he auctioned off merchandise of all kinds. [*He was also a realtor and stock broker.*]

C.E. Gifford & Company [*Charles Ellis Gifford (1841-1895) and Edmund Chace Gifford (1852-1908)*], jeweler on the corner [*at 1 South Main Street*]; Charles A. Baker (1833-1919), the druggist; Charles H. Dean (1821-1882) [*"dry goods"*]; Iram Smith Sr. (1897-1985) [*"dry goods"*]; the "What Is It" variety store; Henry Slade Buffinton (1825-1895) carpets [*and "dry goods"*]; Robert Adams (1816-1900) [*"bookseller and stationer"*]; Wadsworth, Williams & Co. the first large dry goods store [*J. Wadsworth, John W. Williams (born circa 1847), and Henry Strassman]; Louis J. Noros (born 1825), ["books, periodicals, &c."*]; and on the corner of Anawan Street was Borden, Almy & Company [*Andrew Jackson Borden (1822-1892), William M. Almy (1821-1885), and Theodore Dwight Weld Wood (1836-1914)*], furniture dealers and undertakers. [*Andrew J. Borden has gone down in history as much more than the business partner of Messrs. Almy and Wood. On the morning of August 4, 1892, he and his wife, née Abby Durfee Gray (1826 -1892) were brutally murdered at their home on Second Street in Fall River. Borden's daughter Lizzie was tried and acquitted for the crimes; the perpetrator was never found.*]

On the opposite corner [*at 45 South Main Street*] was Westgate, Baldwin

& Company [*Abner L. Westgate (1810-1889), Daniel W. Baldwin (1821-1896), and Thomas Briggs Waring (1839-1910), "furniture manufacturer and undertaker"*]. Afterwards [*the partnership was dissolved, and*] the firms [*operated independently as*] Baldwin and Waring [*Brothers*] in the same business. [*The Waring brothers were the aforementioned Thomas B. Waring, and Henry Waring (1830-1908).*] There was great rivalry between these firms, so much so that families divided on the issue of which one should be patronized.

Later James McDermott (1842-1889), a very fine looking man, opened an undertaker's establishment on Spring Street; opposite Saint Mary's Church [*Roman Catholic*]. He purchased a magnificent hearse with six urns on top equipped with tall waving plumes. With two or four handsome black horses, plumes in the bridles, and draped in heavy fringed nets, the funeral cortege always paraded through Main Street, Mr. McDermott arrayed in a frock coat, silk hat, black gloves, arms folded across his chest looking neither to the right nor the left was an impressive sight. He never deigned to drive himself, but had the driver beside him arrayed as funereal as [*he was*] himself.

In the case of the funeral of a prominent person, the cortege would be preceded by Saint Mary's Band playing a dirge which added to the impressiveness of the parade.

South of Anawan Street on the west side, the First Methodist Church, where Cherry & Webb Company [*ladies' and misses' ready-to-wear clothing, 139-149 South Main Street*] is located, set back from the street, the stores which you probably remember, were placed in front in the early 1880s. Further south, on part of the lot now occupied by the R. A. McWhirr Company department Store, the Church of the Ascension [*Episcopal*], a little brown structure, was also set back from the street up on a bank. Still further south, the Baptist Temple, which still occupies the same site, was also back from the street before they also erected the present stores. So you will see that for quite a stretch there were very few stores. The Church of the Ascension was next to Charity Lane, so-called, and the R. A. McWhirr Company afterwards covered this with buildings. [*The R.A. McWhirr Company, commonly referred to as "McWhirr's," opened its doors in 1877. In March 1975, Fall River's favorite department store ceased its retail business after ninety-seven years in operation.*]

At the corner of Spring Street was the Saint James Hotel building. [*It was located at 249 and 251 South Main Street and 345 Spring Street. The proprietors, George H. Kelly (1845-1912) and James Sutcliffe (1844 -1917)*]

43. Advertisement for McDermott Brothers, Furnishing Undertakers, 1880.

44. Church of the Ascension, South Main Street, early 1870s.

45. Temple Baptist Society (Baptist Temple), 85 South Main Street, circa 1888.

were in partnership for thirty-five years. The hotel was destroyed by fire in 1900.] Robert Manning Gibbs (1850-1914) [*known as R. Manning Gibbs*], had a drug store in this building.

The Borden Block was erected in the early 1870s and the Academy of Music was opened in 1876. As you know, the Theodore Thomas Orchestra was the first attraction. [*Theodore Christian Friedrich Thomas (1835-1905), a native of Germany, was a virtuoso violinist and orchestral conductor, credited as the first renowned member of that profession in America. Among his stellar list of accomplishments, was the founding, in 1891, of the Chicago Symphony Orchestra; he served as its music director from that date until his death.*]

The demolishment of the old buildings on the site and the construction of the basement consumed many months, as a great ledge of granite was uncovered and had to be blasted out and removed. You have no doubt noticed the carvings on the stone work of the building. This was all done by hand after the stone was put in place and for many months, skilled sculptors on swing stages, with awnings to protect them from the sun, were engaged in this work. The building itself was really built around the Academy of Music, as the primary idea seemed to be to construct a theatre which should surpass anything in this part of the country, and in fact the stage was the largest in New England, with the single exception of the Boston Theatre. [*Thomas R. Burrell's first association with the Academy of Music was on opening night in January, 1876, when he was in charge of the coat room for the first event to be performed on its stage; Burrell was fifteen at the time. His involvement with the theatre was to continue; in 1885, The Fall River Directory lists his occupation as "agent, Borden block, and manager, Academy of Music." He was to continue in that capacity for the next three years. His reminiscences of the triumphs and tragedies behind the scenes at the Academy were documented in his manuscript, "The Academy of Music in the Old Days," presented at the Fall River Historical Society in 1939.*]

At the corner of South Main and Pleasant Streets, the first floor was fitted for banking rooms, and also the second floor, afterwards occupied by the Commercial Club [*organized in 1880*].

The corner of Pleasant and Second Streets duplicated this. That is, these two corners were planned to accommodate four banks, two on the street floor and two on the second floor, equipped with stone vaults with steel doors. As a matter of fact the Metacomet National Bank, which had been located below the hill opposite the [*American*] Print Works, [*on Anawan Street, corner of Water Street,*] moved into the Main Street corner and remained there until 1886, when they erected the building on Bedford Street that was destroyed in the fire of 1928.

[*On February 2, 1928, at 6:27 p.m., an alarm was called in to the Fall River Fire Department after employees at the* Fall River Herald News *reported seeing flickering light in the window of Mill No. 2 of the Pocasset Manufacturing Company, a mill complex situated across the street from the newspaper offices. The fire was believed to have started when oily rags left near a heater ignited. It spread rapidly, engulfing the oil-soaked floors of the mill building. By the time the conflagration was over, six blocks in the heart of Fall River's business district were destroyed. It was four days before the last of the fire apparatus would be removed from the devastated area. Among the buildings declared a total loss were: Mill Nos. 1 through 4 of the Pocasset Manufacturing Company; the Granite Block; Temple Beth El; the Rialto and Premier Theatres; the Union, Citizens, Massasoit-Pocasset, and Metacomet Banks; and the Wilbur and Mohican Hotels. A considerable number of other buildings were among those left as smoldering rubble, including the supposedly fire-proof Buffington Building that housed the office and exhibit room of the Fall River Historical Society. Their entire collection was lost, except for a selection of important items stored in a safe, which survived the inferno unscathed.]*

John Milton Deane (1840-1914) [*"grocer"*] was forced to move in [*at 14 South Main Street*] before the Borden Block was really completed, as his former store [*at 41 Bedford Street*] was to be torn down to make way for the construction of the Post Office [*Custom House*] Building.

James F. Westgate had died and his [*hardware*] store at [*1 North Main Street, at*] the corner of Bedford and Main Streets, was to be remodeled for the Massasoit National Bank.

46. John M. Deane, dry goods, 90 and 94 South Main Street. The reverse of the photograph is inscribed: "Inside John M. Deane Store. Man at right is Martin Joseph Fahey (1897-c.1974)."

47. "West side of South Main Street, from Pocasset Street southerly"; the façade of Preble Brothers, Boots & Shoes, is clearly evident.

48. Trade card for Preble Brothers, Boots & Shoes, 1880s.

Daniel Stillwell moved [*his "hardware and cutlery" store*] from the other corner to Flint's Exchange [*Flint's Block, 45 Pleasant Street, corner of Third Street*] as his building was to be demolished to make room for the Durfee Block [*on North Main Street, corner of Central Street*]. Frank [*Francis*] E. Trafton (1835-1897) was head clerk for Westgate, and Byron W. Anthony (1848-1929) for Stillwell. They organized the hardware firm of Trafton & Anthony and they, too, moved in [*at 12 South Main Street*] before the completion of the Borden Block.

Preble Brothers [*William Henry Preble (1844-1930) and Humphrey Preble (1842-1928), "boots and shoes"*], moved from the west side to the east side, and were next to John M. Deane. While one store afterwards occupied by Preble Brothers was vacant, it was fitted up as a theatre to attract the patronage from the low-priced theatres, which were drawing trade from the Academy of Music. Vaudeville shows were the leading features, although they were then called variety shows.

Denman Thompson [*stage name of Henry Denman Thompson (1833-1911), an American playwright and actor*] appeared here a number of times in the skit "Josh Whitcomb" [*that he wrote and first performed in 1875*]. It was afterwards developed by him into the play *The Old Homestead*, which became a classic and earned a number of fortunes for Mr. Thompson, who still played the leading role of Josh Whitcomb. [*Written by Thompson in 1885, The Old Homestead was first performed in Boston, Massachusetts, in 1886, to critical acclaim. The leading character, Josh Whitcomb, was contemporaneously characterized as a "New Hampshire hayseed" who travels to the "big city."*]

Leander Davenport Wilbur [*L.D. Wilbur & Company, "merchant tailors"*] and William Hoar Ashley [*Wm. H. Ashley & Company, "clothing"*] were north of the Main Street entrance, and John Henry Boone, the [*merchant*] tailor, and a man named Boas, men's furnishings, were south [*David S. Boas, "Hats, caps, and gents' furnishing goods"*].

Lincoln, Kelley & Bennett occupied a double store south of the entrance, with a stairway to the second floor where Hiram [*Judson*] Bennett (1844-1891) displayed pianos and gave music lessons.

Two dance halls, Waverly Hall at the south end of the building [*at 48 Borden Block*], and Trojan Hall much larger at the north end were included in the lay-out. Trojan Hall was afterwards leased to Bristol County and made over to accommodate the Superior Court.

On the Pleasant Street side, at the entrance on one side [*at 1 Borden Block*] was the Western Union Telegraph Company, and on the other

D. S. BOAS,

HATTER

AND DEALER IN

GENTS' FURNISHING GOODS,

28 South Main St.,

BORDEN BLOCK.

Next to Kinsley Express Office,

FALL RIVER.

Agency for Riverside Steam Laundry Co.

Don't Look on the Other Side.

49. Trade card for D.S. Boas, Hatter & Dealer in Gents' Furnishing Goods, 28 South Main Street, 1880s.

side was Tuttle, Milne & Company, cotton brokers [*Elias A. Tuttle, John Cruickshank Milne, George A. Milne (1853-1912), and Patrick J. Hurley (1848-1927), "cotton and print cloths."*] The present chairman of the Fall River Board of Assessors [*in 1936*], James Albert Griffiths, was a telegraph boy and delivered messages from this office.

On the Second Street corner, Ballou and Aldrich, [*William Bowen Ballou (1859-1948) and Earl Hulbert Aldrich (1861-1911)*] at one time Aldrich & Wells [*Earl H. Aldrich and James Henry Wells (1841-1908); the latter was always referred to as J. Henry Wells*], mill supplies and hardware, were located.

Before the building was fully completed and the store windows had been put in place, a serious strike of mill operatives took place. A protest parade formed at the South Park and marched down South Main Street, some of the marchers carrying banners and placards, and some with poles on which were loaves of bread and pasteboard signs: "Give Us Bread or Give Us Blood."

James [*Franklin*] Davenport (1832-1885) was mayor [*from 1874 to 1877*], and Andrew [*Robeson*] Wright (1832-1899), city marshal; the alarm was given and quickly a line of police was formed in front of City Hall, and the mayor and Marshal Wright mounted an express wagon, Wright with a revolver in each hand. Mayor Davenport read the riot act and ordered them to disperse in the name of the law. They broke ranks, ran into the open stores of the Borden Block, and a shower of stones and broken brick and mortar poured forth. Wright ordered his men into the fray and, as men were found with missiles in their hands, they were seized and rushed through the street to the Central Police Station on Granite Street.

50. A staged hazing ceremony for the fraternal organization, Independent Order of the Sons of Malta. Depicted are Darius "King" Wilbur, kneeling, and William "Ice Bill" Durfee, with the paddle.

[*In January 1875, an exclusively male meeting of weavers voted to accept the recent twenty percent wage reduction under protest. As Philip T. Silvia Jr., PhD, in his book,* Victorian Vistas: Fall River, 1865–1885 *wrote: "Though this decision seemingly spiked strike enthusiasm, the force of militant feminism was about to be unleashed." Their female counterparts, convinced that time was ripe, boldly decided on a work stoppage, forcing their male comrades to reconsider and join them.*

In early February, weavers walked off their jobs and the designated mills were emptied when other departments soon followed. The strike intensified on March 1, when employees quit three additional mills.

Because of improved cloth prices, mill agents were eager to resume operations; in a secret meeting with the strike committee they agreed to the wage hike provided loss of face with the public was avoided. Workers returned to the mills, and after a short time lag, began receiving the ten percent increments in April. Silvia continued: "Thus the struggle precipitated by a group of determined women concluded successfully."

Nevertheless, the Board of Trade soon announced that, because of a renewed decline in market prices, the ten percent the workers had regained would be withdrawn. In response, the operatives decided that a new work stoppage would relieve the glutted market, create new demand, higher prices, and higher wages.

According to Silvia, "Thus began 'the Great Vacation', with 15,000 factory hands supporting the union perspective by spending the month of August away from the mills. . . . Numerous employees whose families were soon reduced to a living scale of abject poverty became disenchanted and anxious to terminate their 'vacation.'" But, the manufacturers' response was: "You took four weeks' vacation for your purposes, we will now take four more for our own."

The manufacturers only agreed to reopen the gates on September 27, stipulating that returning employees would be forced to sign an "iron clad" statement repudiating unionism. Despite hardship, many workers continued to stay out on the 27th, forming a delegation to march on City Hall and a mayor unsympathetic to their request for a government food subsidy.

In a dramatic confrontation, the mayor, accompanied by the city marshal brandishing a pair of revolvers, demanded that the crowd disperse. They didn't immediately comply and, at the mayor's command, the police charged into the crowd with their billies. Silvia stated, "A little pounding quickly cleared the streets and ended this labor defiance in a thuddingly terminal fashion. . . . Capital had reasserted control, and its unwillingness to brook trade union opposition had been witnessed by all. The magnitude of victory was manifest late in the year when no employee dared to speak out against the manufacturers for hanging posters in every city cotton textile mill announcing yet another wage reduction."]

It has been said that if you stand at Turk's Head in Providence, Rhode Island, [*at the corner of Westminster and Weybosset Streets*] any day from eleven o'clock until two o'clock, you will see almost every prominent man in Rhode Island pass that point. In the period we have selected for this paper, standing at the four corners in Fall River, [*the junction of*] Bedford, Central, and Main Streets, let us note the passers-by.

At the stroke of twelve noon, Stephen Davol (1807-1888), treasurer of the Pocasset Manufacturing Company, whose office was then in the Granite Block, steps to the sidewalk and walks to his home on North Main Street, the house now [*in 1936*] occupied by Dr. John H. Doyle (1878-1965), and at exactly one o'clock he will be seen stepping from the sidewalk into the entrance to his office. Day after day, with no variation in time.

51. William Carr.

52. William Borden Durfee Sr.

53. William Mowry Hawes.

54. Hon. Robert Henry.

55. George F. Mellen.

From below the hill up Central Street came William Carr (1821-1893), treasurer of the Fall River Steamboat Company; "Gas Bill Durfee," [*William B. Durfee (1832-1896), so-called because he was the superintendent of the Fall River Gas Works Company*]; Robert C. Brown (1809-1900), treasurer of the Fall River Iron Works Company; William Mowry Hawes (1833-1898), over three hundred pounds in weight, always smiling and bowing right and left to his friends; Jim [*James P.*] Hillard (1821-1892), Superintendent of the American Linen Company; Jonathan Hilliard (1818-1885), James Henry (1805-1893), Robert Henry (1833-1914), and John P. Henry (1847-1901), all connected with the American Print Works [*employed respectively as: "superintendent of machinery"; "superintendent"; "assistant superintendent"; and "color mixer"*]; William Davenport (1824-1899) and Charles E[*dwin*] Case (1826-1920), also American Print Works overseers; dapper little Harry [*Henry Jackson*] Jernegan (1856-1933), agent of the Clyde Line [*"Clyde's Philadelphia and New England Steamship Line from Fall River to Philadelphia, Direct"*] well-dressed and always crowned with a silk hat; and Andrew Luscomb (1833-1903), three-hundred-and-fifty pounds, pausing every fifty feet or so to rest.

Along Main Street comes "Diamond Billy Potter" [*William Sydney Potter 1847-1908*], bookkeeper at the Flint Mills, round as a barrel, wearing a short mouse-colored overcoat, and sporting a silk hat, diamond stud, and diamond ring. At the mill, the silk hat was always parked atop of the safe, carefully protected by a clean sheet of white paper.

Louis Robeson (1844-1913), treasurer of the Robeson Mills, tall, handsome, the type of an English Aristocrat trailed by a handsome brindle, English bull dog.

From the north comes "Jehovah Jim" [*James S.*] Anthony (1824-1904), white hair and beard, cape overcoat, hand across his chest, a striking figure reminding one of pictures of Henry Wadsworth Longfellow. [*James S. Anthony first appears in* The Fall River Directory *for 1864 as a "soapboiler." In the following directory, he is listed as the proprietor of James S. Anthony & Co., working with Peter C. White (1813-1886). The association with White lasted until 1871; Anthony continued on his own until 1874, when Reuben Hargraves (1834-1905) and Thomas Hargraves (1836-1904) entered the firm. Within four years, Anthony retired, and the remaining partners founded Hargraves Manufacturing Company.*]

One saw Captain James Brady, with his false leg, carrying a stout cane. On Memorial Day mornings, Captain Brady would have a horse ready in a yard back of the harness shop and I remember helping my father strap him to the saddle preparatory to his participating in the parade. We were instructed by our teacher, Phebe P. Huntsman (1841-1883), of blessed memory, to always touch our caps whenever we met the Captain, and he never failed to return it in true military style, greatly to our pride and satisfaction.

Few know the story of the Captain's injuries as he once told it to me. At the head of his company [*Company G., Twenty-Sixth Massachusetts Infantry*], he was ordered to charge a group of Confederates concealed behind a growth of bushes; unknown to them it protected a masked battery, and as they charged they were received by a galling fire, and the Captain was hurled into the air struck by a charge of shrapnel. His limb swelled so quickly that his clothing, tightening, partially stopped the flow of blood. Confederate surgeons started to examine him when the Union soldiers recharged and drove the enemy to cover. The Confederate surgeons took his watch, sword, jack-knife, and even his cap, and ran. He was taken to the hospital and, when able to travel, came North by easy stages. One night he was placed in the parlor of a southern tavern propped up in a chair. He could not sleep and just after daybreak, orderlies rushed to the front of the house with horses, and at the same time officers came clattering down the stairs, mounted the horses, and rushed off. The Captain said he knew something unusual was happening, but not what; he learned later that it was Phil Sheridan [*General Philip Henry Sheridan (1831-1881)*] starting on his twenty-mile ride to save the day at Winchester, [*Virginia*]. The Captain reached home and afterwards was carried on a stretcher to the Troy Cotton & Woolen Manufactory to cast his vote for the re-election of President Abraham Lincoln. Was Miss Huntsman a militarist in instructing us to salute a man who had had an experience like that?

George F. Mellen (1853-1901), in the early 1870s, drove an old, old white horse attached to a rattle-trap express wagon belonging to Edward M. Pierce (1823-1888), from whom he learned the carpenter's trade. Mr. Mellen's father [*Aaron M. Mellen (1826-1911)*] was foreman for Mr. Pierce, and George worked on the Charles Osborne Shove (1823-1875) house on Highland Avenue as an ordinary carpenter. But, within a period of ten years, he became the leading promoter of Fall River with wide financial connections outside of the city and instead of driving the old white horse came to business in a closed carriage drawn by a pair of horses driven by a coachman. [*George F. Mellen was "noted as one of the most enterprising and energetic businessmen ever known" in Fall River. After retiring from carpentry, he opened a real estate and insurance office, following which* *he established, Mellen & Stafford, a private banking and brokerage firm, with Foster Manning Stafford (1842-1882). In 1880, he founded Forest Hill Gardens, a hotel, resort, and amusement park on North Main Street. According to a contemporary souvenir booklet: Forest Hill Gardens was comprised of "twenty acres of land, situated about two and a half miles from City Hall and was accessible by railway, horsecars and steamboat ... fitted up at the expense of $250,000 for the superior accommodations for the public ... on a scale fitting to the demands of the pleasure-loving public." Among Mellen's other investments was the Mellen House, a fashionable hotel located on North Main Street in Fall River.]*

Joe Ward [*was*] the town crier, a man with two club feet who stood on the corner ringing a large bell, crying the news of the day, and announcing the bargain sales and auctions.

Abraham Bowen (1803-1889), with his gray shawl wrapped around his shoulders crying, "He be, He be," and delivering his little paper, the FALL RIVER ALL SORTS and TIVERTON ADVERTISER, in which he had recorded his opinion of the topics of the day. [*The* Fall River All Sorts and Tiverton Advertiser, *published by Abraham Bowen, was circulated on Saturday mornings. It is unclear as to when the newspaper was founded, but it is present in the first* Fall River Directory *published in 1853. Its motto: "Bound to no sect, ruled by no party."*]

Taffy Harry [*was dressed*] in his white uniform, [*carrying*] a broad tray [*that*] was suspended from his neck, on which was displayed his home-made taffy put up in little paper cones—five cents a cone.

Peter Hughes (1826-1892), who carried a small piece of metal in his hand with which he would strike an iron lamp post to attract attention, and removing his glasses, attached to a wide, black silk cord, delivered his lecture on the state of the Nation, always in exactly the same words. [*Peter Hughes first appears in* The Fall River Directory *in 1870, listed as a "laborer"; the* United States Federal Census *for that year records his age as thirty-one years. For the next twenty-two years, his occupation remains unchanged.*]

I remember Joe [*Joseph*] Bruck (1856-1912), oil salesman for Robert Knight Remington (1826-1886). Joe was an ambitious fellow and a ready talker. He patented a device for piping a building for oil and, by a syphon effect, draw the oil to the burner from which it was confidently stated it could be lighted the same as gas. He organized a company and sold considerable stock. A certain doctor, now dead, subscribed for some of the stock. The device was not a success. Later, this doctor was in the

South Station in Boston, Massachusetts, and having a long wait for his train, called at the news stand and asked for an exciting book. The lady in attendance said she had a new book which she had just read, Rudyard Kipling's *The Light That Failed.* "That's not new, I bought it years ago from Joe Bruck and it cost me fifteen hundred dollars."

Dr. Félix Victor Marissal (1824-1881) a little French physician, clad in a fur-lined overcoat and carrying a gold-headed cane, esteemed as very skillful and frequently called in consultation. He had a habit of raising his cane in the air and calling "hands-up" to the boys as they passed on the street.

56. Robert Knight Remington. "Robert Knight Remington, the founder of Borden & Remington [dealers in calico printers', dyers', and woolen manufacturers' supplies] will be remembered by all who knew him because of his personal charm and his many-sided character."

57. Rev. Edward Murphy. "Good old Father Edward Murphy of St. Mary's Church."

Good old Father Edward Murphy (1811-1887) of Saint Mary's Church [*Cathedral of Saint Mary of the Assumption, Roman Catholic*], everybody's friend, driving through Main Street with his Sexton, Lawrence Phelan (1850-1894), holding the reins over his fast stepping horse.

M[*oses*] Frank Pike (1837-1882), [*the*] city messenger, carrying his little black and tan dog in his arms and equipped with a small bottle of Jamaica Ginger in each upper vest pocket. [*Jamaica Ginger, also called "Jake," was a nineteenth-century patent medicine with an extremely high alcohol content, typically from 70% to 80%.*]

Dr. John J. Solomon, the Indian herb doctor [*"physician, 92 Bedford Street"*] with his medicine bag – he was a full-blooded Indian with coal black curls hanging down over his coat collar. [*John J. Solomon (1844-1921) was consistently identified as "mulatto" in the Federal Census. Born in Attleboro, Massachusetts, he was the son of James M. Solomon (1812-1889), a self-professed "Indian Doctor," and his wife, née Rebecca A. Parker*

(1821-1886). A Civil War veteran, he served with Company C., Forty-Seventh Massachusetts Infantry, in the capacity of Assistant Surgeon.]

Dan [*Daniel J.*] Warden (circa 1835-1887), his face seamed with innumerable scars, accompanied by his two ferocious blood hounds. [*Daniel J. Warden was a "horse dealer" in Fall River.*]

Joseph Shove (1818-1893), [*was*] the little old undertaker of Somerset, who drove a one-horse hearse with full length glass sides. Mr. Shove was in the habit of doing his Fall River shopping with this equipage and was often seen driving home with his bundles packed on the floor of the hearse.

At night, a quack doctor selling Flagg's Instant Relief, perched on an express wagon at the corner of Market Square, flaring torches at each end. He would select the deafest man he could find, park him in the crowd, and then call for some person so afflicted; his confederate would climb up, the doctor would rub some of his liniment on his ears, whisper to him, ask if he could hear, receive a nod in reply, pronounce him cured, and offer his remedy at one dollar a bottle, and it was astonishing how many bottles were sold. [*Flagg's Instant Relief was developed in 1853 by patent medicine manufacturer and promoter Edward H. Flagg (1823-1910). Sold by hired agents across the United States, the product was billed as a pain killer and miraculous "cure-all." Rev. Michael Bernard Buckley (1831-1872), a contemporary Irish diarist, then touring America, wrote of the product: "The wonder of this world, this miracle of Pharmacopeia, is entitled 'Flagg's Instant Relief' and is sold for the ridiculously small sum of one dollar per bottle. Will it be believed that thousands are gulled by the blarney of these itinerant musical medicine vendors, and the great unseen Flagg realizes a gigantic fortune by the credulity of an innocent public? No less than twelve equipages of this kind do the work of advertising and selling his 'Instant Relief'; and it is said fifty dollars a day is about the amount received by each troupe, an enormous receipt in return for a trifling outlay."*]

Often late in the evening a quartette or sextette, Velona Winant Haughwout (1851-1934), John W. Pritchard (1844-1891) Jimmie [*James H.*] Ricketson (1857-1907) Parker Borden (1828-1893), Harry [*Henry J.*] Jernegan, Rienzi W. Thurston (1851-1914), Walter D. Terry (1852-1927), Charlie [*Charles Austin*] Bonney (1819-1879), Louis Person Davis (1849-1883), and men with voices of that caliber would walk through Main Street singing familiar songs, and if there are singers today who can surpass those men in rendering "Down In A Coal Mine," "Old Black Joe," or "Massa's In De Cold Ground," I do not know them.

"Down In A Coal Mine"
Lyrics written in 1872
by
Joseph Bryan Geoghegan (1816-1889)

I am a jovial collier lad; and blithe as blithe can be,
For let the times be good or bad, they're all the same to me;
'Tis little of the world I know and care less for its ways,
For where the dog star never glows, I wear away my days.

Down in a coal mine underneath the ground,
Where a gleam of sunshine never can be found;
Digging dusky diamonds all the season round,
Down in a coal mine underneath the ground.

My hands are horny hard and black, with working in the vein,
And like the clothes upon my back, my speech is rough and plain;
Well if I stumble with my tongue, I've one excuse to say,
'Tis not the colliers heart that's wrong. 'Tis th' head that goes astray.

At ev'ry shift be't soon or late, I haste my bread to earn,
And anxiously my kindred wait and watch for my return;
For Death that levels all alike whate'er their rank may be,
Amid the fire and damp may strike, and fling his darts at me.

How little do the great ones care, who sit at home secure,
What hidden dangers colliers dare, what hardships they endure;
The very fires their manions boast to cheer themselves and wives,
Mayhap were kindled at the cost, of jovial colliers lives.

Then cheer up lads and make ye much, of ev'ry joy ye can,
But let your mirth be always such as best becomes a man;
How ever Fortune turns about, we'll still be jovial souls,
For what would England be without, the lads that look for coals.

❦

"Old Black Joe"
Lyrics written in 1853
by
Stephen Collins Foster (1826-1864)

Gone are the days when my heart was young and gay,
Gone are my friends from the cotton fields away,
Gone from the earth to a better land I know,
I hear their gentle voices calling, "Old Black Joe."

I'm coming, I'm coming, for my head is bending low;
I hear those gentle voices calling, "Old Black Joe."

Why do I weep when my heart should feel no pain?
Why do I sigh that my friends come not again,
Grieving for forms now departed long ago.
I hear their gentle voices calling, "Old Black Joe."

I'm coming, I'm coming, for my head is bending low;
I hear those gentle voices calling, "Old Black Joe."

Where are the hearts once so happy and so free?
The children so dear that I held upon my knee,
Gone to the shore where my soul has longed to go.
I hear those gentle voices calling, "Old Black Joe."

I'm coming, I'm coming, for my head is bending low:
I hear those gentle voices calling, "Old Black Joe."

❧❧

"Massa's In De Cold Ground"
Lyrics written in 1852
by
Stephen Collins Foster (1826-1864)

Round de meadows am a-ringing
De darkeys' mournful song, Wile de mocking-bird am singing,
Happy as de day am long.
Where de ivy am creeping
O'er de grassy mound,
Dare old massa am a-sleeping,
Sleeping in de cold, cold ground.

Down in de cornfield
Hear dat mournful sound:
All de darkeys' am a-weeping –
Massa's in de cold, cold ground.

Down in de cornfield
Hear dat mournful sound:
All de darkeys' am a-weeping –
Massa's in de cold, cold ground.

When de autumn leaves were falling,
When de days were cold,
'Twas hard to hear old massa calling,
Cayse he was so weak and old.
Now de orange tree am blooming
On de sandy shore,
Now de summer days am coming,
Massa nebber calls no more.

Down in de cornfield
Hear dat mournful sound:
All de darkeys' am a-weeping –
Massa's in de cold, cold ground.

Down in de cornfield
Hear dat mournful sound:
All de darkeys' am a-weeping –
Massa's in de cold, cold ground.

Massa made de darkeys' love him,
Cayse he was so kind,
Now dey sadly weep above him,
Mournful cayse he leave them behind.
Cayse de tear drops flow,
I try to drive away my sorrow
Pickin on de old banjo.

Down in de cornfield
Hear dat mournful sound:
All de darkeys' am a weeping –
Massa's in de cold, cold ground.

Down in de cornfield
Hear dat mournful sound:
All de darkeys' am a weeping –
Massa's in de cold, cold ground.

And if I in writing this imperfect paper, if you in listening patiently to its reading, and if the Fall River Historical Society in placing it with its records, have lifted these names from the list of forgotten men, I feel with you, that we are well repaid.

A Businessman's Reminiscences of Fifty Years

In an historical address, it is usual to speak of the founders of a city or of a country, but in all history there has come a time when some man or men were called upon to preserve that which the fathers had established. It was so in our national history – a Washington founded our government – but the time came when a Lincoln saved it from destruction.

So, in a sense, the men of a century ago established our city [*of Fall River*] upon a firm foundation, but there came a time when men of courage and determination were called upon to preserve what men of former generations had established.

It is of those men [*and women*] and of those times that I am to speak, of men only with whom I came in contact at the beginning of whatever career I may have had in business.

While these men became very wealthy, it is well worthy of note that they had thought of other things besides the mere accumulation of money. If you are at all familiar with the institutions of the city [*of Fall River*], you are aware that almost without exception, the men who I am to mention were actively interested in every one of them during their lives. Regardless of what they may have willed, they devoted a share of their lives to the development of institutions consecrated to the welfare of their fellow men.

For example: You cannot write the history of the Young Men's Christian Association without mentioning the name of Robert Knight Remington (1826-1886).

You cannot write the history of the [*Fall River*] Deaconess Home, the Italian Methodist Church, or the African Methodist Episcopal Church without mentioning the name of John Dexter Flint (1826-1907). [*Fall River Deaconess Home, which is still in existence as of this writing, is a private, community-based agency whose services include residential education and pre-independent living programs for young women ages 11 to 22.*]

You cannot write the history of Swansea, Massachusetts, without mentioning the names of Jonathan Slade (1815-1900) and William Lawton Slade (1817-1895).

You cannot write the history of the Fall River Women's Union without mentioning the name of Mrs. William Henry Jennings [*née Annie Borden Chase (1841-1924). Fall River Women's Union was one of the earliest social welfare organizations in the city, which benefited women who were reliant only upon themselves for support; the organization is still in existence today and assists various nonprofit agencies.*]

You cannot write the history of Adamsville, Rhode Island, without mentioning the name of Abraham Manchester (1851-1919). He fed the hungry, he clothed the naked, he visited the sick, and on one occasion at least, he officiated at the burial of the dead.

You cannot write the history of the Fall River District Nursing Association without mentioning the name of William Buffum Hawes (1862-1932).

You cannot write the history of the Fall River High School Alumni Association without mentioning the name of William B. Hawes.

You cannot write the history of the schools of Fall River without mentioning the name of Mary (Brayton) Durfee Young (1814-1891).

You cannot write the history of the Fall River Public Library without mentioning the name of Leontine Lincoln (1846-1923).

You cannot write the history of the Salvation Army without mentioning the name of James Boyd Harley (1835-1902).

You cannot write the history of the Boys Club of Fall River without mentioning the name of Matthew Chaloner Durfee Borden (1842-1912).

All of these [*individuals*] lived and labored for the better things which we have in our city today.

My personal recollection of Fall River business and Fall River businessmen runs back to 1878, when I entered the employ of the Fall River National Bank as a messenger, at a salary of $150.00 a year, or $12.50 per month. This monthly salary was not paid to me in cash, but a deposit slip was made out and the amount credited to me in the books. This was explained to me as being a lesson in banking, but I always felt that it was done so that the bank might hold my money a few days longer than would have been the case if payment had been made in cash.

I was sixteen years old at the time and greatly interested in the men who visited the bank, noting their conversation, peculiarities, and the

58. Thomas Richmond Burrell Sr., 1883.

evidence many of them gave of unusual business acumen, keenness of thought, and courage in time of great business stress.

While this article will no doubt appear as somewhat rambling, it may, I hope, give new and perhaps interesting facts regarding men who have been prominent in the [Fall River] community.

Where it would seem that no harm may ensue I shall use names, believing that thereby a greater interest may be excited and the outstanding characteristics of these men may be more clearly presented.

No longer young in years myself, but young, I trust, in spirit, I hope I may not leave the impression of comparing the men of the past years with those of the present to the detriment of our leading men of the present day. We had weak men, no doubt, in those times, but we certainly had men of vision and men of undaunted courage, strong in their opinions and willing to act on their judgment, and to back their opinions with their money and with their credit.

We who have lived and walk the streets of Fall River should not forget those who made the city, who built the mills – which paid great dividends up to a few years ago – and gave employment to tens of thousands of people, making it possible for them to build homes and bring up their children in comfort and comparative plenty.

With this preface, please understand that this is not an historical paper in the strict sense of the word but an intimate and, I believe, quite accurate picture of personalities who left an impression upon their fellow citizens, which should not be allowed to fade from the memory of those who knew them, or as a lesson to those who must follow them in the conduct of the affairs of the city which we love so well.

❧✕❧

Ferdinand H. Gifford (1838-1914) was cashier of the Fall River National Bank, Charles Bennett Cook (1850-1929), assistant cashier, William Lindsey Jr. (1858-1922), was the teller, and Thomas R. Burrell Sr. (1861-1953) [the author] was messenger.

The other [bank] messengers of the same period were: Frank Linden Andrews (1862-1946) at the First National Bank; Rodolphus N. Allen (1859-1940) at the Massasoit National Bank; William Francis Winters (1860-1919) at the Pocasset National Bank; Omer Elton Borden (1854-1927) at the Second National Bank; Charles M. Freeborn (1862-1940) at the Fall River Savings Bank; Bryant Chapin (1859-1927) at the Union Savings

Bank; and Peter S. Henry (1853-1913) at the Metacomet National Bank.

The Directors of the Fall River National were Guilford H. Hathaway (1808-1895), Richard Baxter Borden (1834-1906), John Palmer Slade (1824-1902), Isaac Borden (1838-1903), and Ferdinand H. Gifford.

All of the officers, clerks and directors are dead [*at the time of this writing*] with one exception, myself.

I was promoted to teller when William Lindsey resigned, and Henry Palmer became messenger when I resigned. Mr. Frederick "Fred" Ezekiel Bemis (1869-1939) became messenger and is the only connecting link between the old and the new.

59. Ferdinand H. Gifford. "His outstanding characteristic was his strict integrity."

Ferdinand H. Gifford, cashier of the bank, was in very poor health and frequently was obliged to stay at home for days at a time because of illness. In later years, his health improved and he became president of the bank and died while holding that office.

His outstanding characteristic was his strict integrity. A gentleman, who was a resident of Cambridge, Massachusetts, inherited a large estate, and included in the assets was stock in all the banks in Fall River. He asked Mr. Gifford if he would dispose of this stock for him as he was not familiar with Fall River values; Mr. Gifford did so and sent him the proceeds.

In a few days, a beautiful watch was sent to Mr. Gifford with the thanks of the gentleman for his services. Mr. Gifford was greatly disturbed and returned the gift with a letter stating that he would not accept it from a stockholder in his bank. This was his attitude throughout his business life, and he would not accept the smallest favor from anyone who did business with him.

Richard B. Borden's life spoke for itself; a successful manufacturer, he succeeded by the old-fashioned, conservative, and honest business methods. No one need question where Mr. Borden would stand on any matter, where right and wrong were concerned. He would always be on the side of right and justice.

I saw this where the question of an increase in salary was involved; a small matter, but he did not feel that it was justified. Turning to his associates, he said: "I will step from the room and you can vote this increase, but I cannot approve of it." And from personal ties, he would have felt that he was called upon to vote in favor more than for anyone connected with the institution. But in justice to his own conscience he would not do it.

Guilford H. Hathaway (1808-1895) of Assonet, Massachusetts, was president. He wore an old-style silk hat and a cape overcoat and always a broadcloth suit and top boots. The bank was heated by stoves, and it was Mr. Hathaway's habit to sit in a swivel chair, feet on the stove, chair tilted back, and sleep peacefully, silk hat on head and arms confined within his cape.

One day, all of a sudden, the castors of the chair slipped, his hat rolled on the floor, his feet aloft and his neck cramped against the wall; the three clerks rushing to his assistance finally got him upon his feet, replaced the hat, and partially restored his dignity.

It was his habit to come to Fall River daily on the train, walking from the station to the bank. At noon, he would proceed across the street to

60. Richard Baxter Borden. "He succeeded by the old-fashioned, conservative business methods" and was "always ... on the side of right and justice."

Mason Fisher's bakery and purchase a dozen cookies for his lunch, eating a few and placing the uneaten ones in a drawer of the directors' table for the next and following days.

"Uncle" Abner Slade (1792-1879) of Somerset, Massachusetts, and Captain Joseph Marble (1799-1880), also of Somerset, were directors – very old and feeble. Guilford H. Hathaway, called a "financial undertaker" because of settlement of many estates, was administrator of the estate of Captain Marble, which amounted to $71,000.

While engaged in dusting the bank one day, I found a common grocer's pass-book containing a mass of figures and memoranda, which I quietly put in my pocket. Mr. Hathaway came in and began looking anxiously for something; finally, he asked if I had seen a book which he said was the record of this $71,000 estate. I pretended to search for a large account book, and then drawing the grocer's book from my pocket asked innocently if this could be it – and it was, the only record of receipts and payments of this substantial estate.

Mr. Hathaway was a man of the strictest integrity and his accounts were accepted without question by the Judges of Probate. Among the assets of Captain Marble's estate was a box of watches on which he had

61. Guilford H. Hathaway. "The bank was heated by stoves, and it was Mr. Hathaway's habit to sit in a swivel chair, feet on the stove, chair tilted back, and sleep peacefully, silk hat on his head and arms confined within his cape."

62. William Lawton Slade. "I have not words to express the respect and affection I felt for this man. The soul of honor applies to him if it ever applied to anyone."

made loans to Stephen Shove (1820-1888), a well-known jeweler of the day. Tags were attached to each watch showing how much had been loaned, the total being about $300.00. As the cases of the watches had turned a greenish black we placed a value of $25.00 on the lot.

Isaac Borden (1838-1903), at that time treasurer of the Montaup Mills, was another striking character, with his silk hat, Prince Albert coat, and long white cuffs, nearly covering his hands. He was much younger, but a likable, warm-hearted, and attractive personality.

I would not feel that I could write an article of this kind without mentioning the name of William Lawton Slade (1817-1895).

I have not words to express the respect and affection I felt for this man. At one time a person long since dead had used Mr. Slade in what he felt – and I felt – was a very unjust manner. Mr. Slade was not well and asked me if I would talk the matter over with the party interested. I did so and finding that I would not get any satisfaction told him what I thought

63. Residence of William L. Slade in Somerset, Massachusetts, later occupied by his daughter, Mrs. Hezekiah Anthony Brayton, née Caroline Elizabeth Slade.

of his dealings in very plain language. In giving Mr. Slade an account of the interview, I told what I had said and the words I had used. He paused a moment and said: "I could not have told him that, but I cannot say that I am sorry you did, and I want to thank you."

The soul of honor applies to him if it ever applied to anyone. I had glimpses of an inner spirit, of a sentimental goodness that I have never seen in another person. He lived in the house in Somerset lately occupied in the summer by Mrs. Hezekiah Anthony Brayton, his daughter, [*née Caroline Elizabeth Slade (1846-1928)*].

I called one evening just at sunset and found Mr. Slade sitting on the veranda, weak and feeble from illness. For a moment, he hardly knew me but asked me to sit down beside him. Looking out over the broad green fields running down to the Taunton River upon which the rays of the setting sun were reflected, he placed his hand on mine, and said: "Thomas, I have looked across those fields for seventy years; it has been my heaven on earth. If heaven above is any lovelier than that, it must be a beautiful place."

Will anyone question that the soul of a poet found expression in those words?

64. Mrs. Hezekiah Anthony Brayton (née Caroline Elizabeth Slade.)

65. Slade Farm, Somerset, Massachusetts. "I have looked across those fields for seventy years; it has been my heaven on earth. If heaven above is any lovelier than that, it must be a beautiful place."

I never saw him again. He was soon gathered to his fathers, but those words have lingered in my memory through all these years, and if my hearers tonight forget all the other things of which I have spoken, I believe those words spoken almost in the last hours of Mr. Slade's life will remain with them long after we close this meeting.

I never pass the Slade homestead without looking down over those fields and repeating in thought the beautiful sentiment so beautifully expressed. Mr. Slade lies buried in those fields which he loved so well.

John Palmer Slade (1824-1902) was one of the most active directors and had a faculty of smoothing over rough places in business. He was always smiling and, if he was in any way disturbed, he never showed it in his countenance.

He was a school mate of my father's when they were boys and attended school at the Brayton Point School. His friendship for my father, no doubt, had much to do with my securing the position at the bank.

The firm of John P. Slade & Son [*Realtors, Insurance, and Mortgages*] conducted by his grandson, now [*in 1933*] occupies offices in the new Fall River National Bank building. At the time of which I am speaking, their office was at the northeast corner of the Granite Block. Everett Nelson Slade (1878-1948), grandson of John P. Slade, was a director in the bank.

When I entered the bank fifty-five years ago, the textile business was at a low ebb; mill stocks were selling for almost nothing, and Savings Banks Books at that time were selling at auction at eighty cents on the dollar as the Stay Law had been invoked to prevent any run upon these institutions. As I remember it, a notice of sixty or ninety days was necessary and then only a portion of the deposit could be drawn.

Henry T. Buffington and Francis "Frank" B. Hood (1819-1899) [*Brokers & Auctioneers, 43 Bedford Street*], who had an office at the corner of Pleasant and Second Streets in the Borden Block, held auctions every Wednesday and Saturday. These were attended largely by people from Somerset, Swansea, and Westport, Massachusetts, and from Warren, Rhode Island, who purchased, to the extent of their means, bank books and mill stocks. Many of the well-to-do families in these towns could trace much of their present wealth to the wisdom and courage of these not-so-distant ancestors.

The bank was heated by stoves, and included in the duties of messenger was starting the fires at seven o'clock in the morning, taking the ashes out through a back window, and bringing in a supply of coal for the day.

The morning mail was brought from Providence, Rhode Island, by

66. John Palmer Slade. "He was always smiling and, if he was in any way disturbed, he never showed it in his countenance."

pony express. The contractor I remember best was John Boardman. He met the New York train at the Central Station in Providence with an open Democrat Wagon, loaded on the mail sacks and, changing horses at Warren, Rhode Island, was due to arrive at the local Post Office about nine o'clock. [*A democrat wagon is an open light-weight flatbed ranch wagon with one or two seats, led by one, or sometimes two, horses. The name "democrat"*

67. "Fall River Iron Works Cotton Mill and Chimney." The height of the chimney, above ground, was 350 feet and it was constructed of 1,300,000 bricks.

referred to its availability and the fact that it was easy to handle, and not because of any political designation. A wire basket was often attached to the side for transporting cargo.] In bad weather, he was occasionally late, and sometimes he would come through Main Street covered with snow and his fast horse steaming like a locomotive.

Showing how close some of the mills ran at the time, I have put up pay-rolls and held them under orders until the mail had arrived and the mill had made a deposit to cover the pay-roll. Many times, it was necessary for the treasurer and leading directors to give checks for a few hundred dollars to cover the amount required. This would seem hardly possible but I have seen it done many times.

A few days after I began my duties, the cashier ordered me to go to the office of the Iron Works Company and get the endorsement of Robert Carver Brown (1809-1900), the treasurer, to one of the company's notes and not to fail in securing it.

The office was at the foot of Anawan Street opposite the American Print Works. When I got there, I was told that Mr. Brown had just gone to the Ferry Street Depot to go to Boston, Massachusetts. I ran all the way to the depot and jumped aboard the train which had already started. I

68. Ferry Street Depot, Fall River, Massachusetts.

found Mr. Brown and stated my errand but was informed that he could do nothing, as fountain pens were not known at that time. I asked the conductor if he would hold the train at the Bowenville Station until Mr. Brown could sign his name. He agreed. We borrowed a pen of the station agent and I got the signature.

I made a great hit with Mr. Gifford, the cashier, and I did not register very strongly with Mr. Brown.

We had some peculiar tenants in the old building. One attorney at law, Warren Allds (1850-1925) by name, hired a small office and slept in it. Monday morning, he deposited two dollars, and at noon drew a check for twenty-five cents to buy his dinner. Just before the bank closed, he drew another twenty-five cents for his breakfast. When his deposit got down to fifty cents, he deposited another two dollars. At the end of the month, he said that he had kept a deposit there and, since it was very evident that the bank did not intend to give him its law business, he would withdraw his account and give up his office.

We had a customer named Pearce from Assonet, Massachusetts, who came in and told Mr. Charles B. Cook that he could not meet a payment on a note because he had had bad luck. A lot of cord wood which he had ready to market had burned up and his loss would be at least $200.00. Mr. Cook, in his impressive and serious manner, asked him if he thought it was incendiary. Mr. Pearce said no, he didn't, he thought it was "sot afire."

There were two competing telephone companies, the Bell and the Edison. Some offices had one system and others the other, but very few had both. We were connected with each from necessity but were greatly inconvenienced by the uncertainty of which system a caller might have.

The street railway was under construction and the first horse car was driven from the Bowenville Station, now the Fall River station, to the corner of Bank and North Main Streets. Edward Herbert (1850-1880), who was the president, acted as driver, and George F. Mellen (1853-1901), the treasurer, stood on the back platform acting as conductor.

But it was the men of prominence who came to the bank counter and gathered to discuss the affairs of the institutions in which they were interested, that left a lasting impression upon my young mind.

It was necessary in those times for directors to endorse the notes of the mills, and directors were compelled in order to float any paper to endorse. They were large holders of the stocks and failure to secure loans meant the immediate downfall of a corporation, and the shutting off of the credit of one might mean the collapse of many, and so the placing of ones name

69. Workers constructing the street railway, South Main Street.

upon the notes of one corporation was in a sense the protecting of the credit of all.

One morning, a group – Frank Shaw Stevens (1827-1898), Dr. [*Robert T.*] Davis (1823-1906), Walter Chaloner Durfee (1816-1901), and John Dexter Flint (1826-1907) – met at the bank for this melancholy duty. One made the prediction that the end had come – cloth was selling at three cents a yard and the oft-repeated remark was made that grass would soon grow in the streets.

Mr. Stevens lit a fresh cigar, looked the group over slowly and thoughtfully, and said: "Boys, I have driven six horses on a stage coach in California and I can do it again. You can't break me."

70. Frank Shaw Stevens. He was "undoubtedly one of the strongest characters which Fall River has produced."

As things grew worse, these men came to the conclusion that they must take hold and manage the properties themselves if they were to ever be placed upon their feet. Mr. Stevens made the remark in the bank, "If my money is to be lost I want to know how it is done," and he assumed the treasurership of both the Davol Mills and Mechanics Mills, endorsing the notes and giving his word of honor that they would be paid. Often, I have seen him with his coat off, in his shirt sleeves at the Mechanics Mills, working like a clerk anxious to retain his job.

A delegation of weavers who had a grievance met Mr. Stevens in his office. Before the leader could state his case, Mr. Stevens asked, "Boys, what's the trouble, we ought to be able to fix this matter," and, opening a drawer in his desk, he slowly opened a box of the choice cigars which he always smoked, passed them around, and talked about the business conditions while his guests puffed contentedly away.

When the cigars had been nearly consumed, he passed the box again, and dismissed them making no concessions, but sending the leaders of the agitation back to their fellow operatives sounding the praises of the treasurer as a fine fellow and a square man.

Many pages could be written about Mr. Stevens, who was undoubtedly one of the strongest characters which Fall River has produced. The following anecdote will no doubt be of interest and it was related to me by Mr. Stevens himself.

He always drove a high-stepping well-bred horse, and while he was always accompanied by a driver, he insisted on holding the reins himself when he was in the carriage. In a blinding snow storm, he drove across the Turner Street crossing; the gates not having been lowered as he reached the east track, he saw the gleaming head light of a locomotive on the west track – as quick as a flash he turned the horse north, but the train moved from the west track to the east to approach the station. Mr. Stevens said he spoke to Willie Wellington, his driver, and said: "Willie, this is the end of us."

At the station platform, the train crashed into the buggy, breaking both of the horse's legs on one side of his body, but throwing the buggy with Mr. Stevens and his driver on to the platform unhurt, but of course shocked and frightened. Mr. Stevens walked back to the gate tender and was not any too mild in expressing his thoughts. The next morning he stopped at the little shanty of the gate tender, called the old man out and, pressing a bill into his hand, told him to forget what, in his excitement, he had said the night before.

71. Turner Street crossing. "At the station platform, the train crashed into [*Frank S. Stevens'*] buggy, breaking both the horse's legs on one side of his body, but throwing the buggy with Mr. Stevens and his driver to the platform unhurt."

In a few days, a stranger called at Mr. Stevens home [*in Swansea, Massachusetts*] and introduced himself as an [*insurance*] adjustor for the railroad. Mr. Stevens gave the value of the horse, buggy, and harness as $800.00. The agent said that was alright and said: "Now, Mr. Stevens, what should we give you for the shock and injury to your feelings." Instantly came the reply: "If you gave me the whole road, it would not pay for the injury to my feelings." He thanked the agent for his reasonable settlement, and, when he prepared to depart, Mr. Stevens called him back and said: "You had better make the check $1,000. I think you injured Willie Wellington's feelings two hundred dollars' worth, and I will give that to him."

No two men could have been more unlike than John D. Flint and Frank S. Stevens. Joseph Healy (1828-1901) [*treasurer of the Osborn Mills*], a unique character himself, once stated that, never mind what the circumstances might have been, you could not have made a John D. Flint out of Frank S. Stevens, or a Frank S. Stevens out of John D. Flint. Mr.

Flint, a deeply religious man, Mr. Stevens a man of the world, and yet each respected the other and would make a business agreement without putting pen to paper.

Few men had the confidence in his own judgment and acted upon it as Mr. Flint did. Once convinced that there was an equity remaining in any corporation in which he was interested, he would give it his support, lend it his credit, and rarely failed to bring it through successfully.

When he elected Fred Waterman, [*Frederick Ellsworth Waterman Sr. (1861-1907)*], a young man, treasurer of the Cornell Mills, then heavily in debt, he called him to one side and said: "Young man, we have not elected you to make excuses, we can hire all the men we want to do that. We have hired you to make money and not to explain to us at the end of the quarter or the end of the year why you have not done so." Mr. Waterman told me that this lesson remained with him always and whenever tempted to excuse any mistake, the words of Mr. Flint came back to him in full force, and had a great influence on his whole life.

In those days of which I have spoken, the banks were extremely careful in all their transactions. Mr. Flint had taken the treasurership of the Flint Mills, and the banks had made a strict rule to take nothing but cashier's checks in payment of drafts with bill of lading attached. Certified checks were not used locally at that time. Mr. Flint drove up to the bank in the chaise [*a two-wheel carriage with a hood*] which he always used and presented a Flint Mill check for $3,800 odd dollars in payment of a draft; under instructions by the cashier, he was told that we must have the cash. Without a word, he left the bank, and in a short time returned with a clerk from another bank, and brought in $3,800 in silver dollars in bags which weighted sixty pounds to the thousand.

At another time, he was notified by letter that a $20,000 note of the mill was coming due and the directors had voted that they wished it paid on the due date. He came in and said the Flint Mill could not pay the note, could not hire any new money and he did not propose to try. The cashier, with great firmness, told him that he had no option, the note must be paid. He walked out and did not appear again until the day the note was due. Stepping to the counter and asking for the cashier, he said: "The Flint Mill owes you $20,000 and they cannot pay it. Here is all I can offer you. If this note is not good, no note in the city is good. If you do not accept it, the red flag goes on the Flint Mill today, and when it goes on the Flint Mill, it will go on many more." He laid down a note with thirteen endorsements – all of his directors and all of his brothers. It goes without saying that the note was accepted. The Flint Mill lived and in after years prospered and earned large dividends for its stockholders.

The last time I saw Mr. Flint, he invited me to ride down town with him and, speaking of his advancing age and painful illness, he said: "Well I have had a happy life and I have had plenty to do." He indeed had plenty to do and that, as he stated, had made his life an unusually happy one.

David Mason "D.M." Anthony (1835-1915) was a man who will live long in the memory of those who knew him. His family were all strong Methodists and his checks for the support of the Church were always made payable to the order of "The Gospel." They were passed through the banks and always occasioned comment, but he never varied the form. His father, "Uncle John Anthony," [*Rev. John Anthony (1807-1876)*], owned a market [*on North Main Street*] situated where the Mellen House [*Hotel Mellen*] now stands [*in 1933*] and D.M. worked for him. Not on the corner, which was the residence of Dr. James Mott Aldrich [*eclectic physician*], but next north nearer the site of the Fall River Savings Bank.

72. Residence of David Mason "D.M." Anthony, 116 North Main Street, circa 1875. Mason is standing in the yard at left.

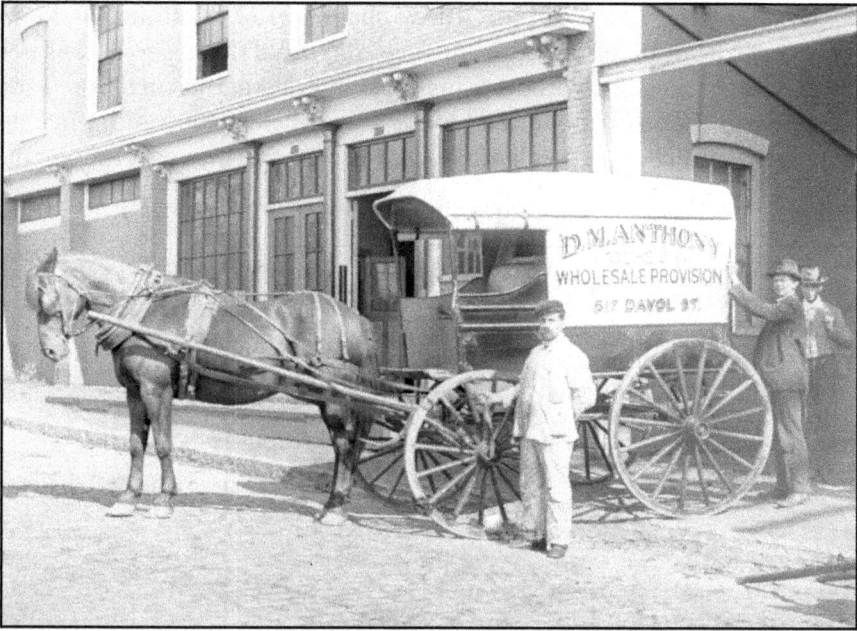

73. Delivery cart for D. M. Anthony, Wholesale Provisions, 1871. "Mr. Anthony, in one of his reminiscent moods, told how he started business for himself."

Mr. Anthony, in one of his reminiscent moods, told how he had started in business for himself. The street floor of the City Hall was divided off into stalls and these were leased to the market men for the sale of meats. D.M. told his father that he had saved $300.00 and had decided to lease a stall in the City Hall and start for himself. "Uncle John" advised him that he had best stay with him and draw his paltry few dollars a week and save his capital. D.M. replied: "Well, father, if I fail I can only be $300.00 poorer or poorer than you are."

The Swift brothers, afterwards the founders of the Swift packing business in Chicago, traveled the Cape [*Cape Cod, Massachusetts,*] buying hogs which they killed and sold as frozen hogs. Mr. Anthony, who had accumulated some money, was called upon many times to guarantee the payment to the farmers for their livestock so that the Swifts might carry on their business. As this increased, he became a partner with them in the provision business under the name of Anthony, Swift & Company, and of course kept his connection with them in the great enterprises which they developed.

Mr. Anthony, like all of the sturdy characters of his time, would go through to the limit for a friend, but once convinced that a person was not strictly on the level, he withdrew his support and had no further use for him. He had endorsed for a friend to the amount of $30,000 and, when he found his confidence had been misplaced, he naturally was very indignant.

SAD ACCIDENT.—On Saturday afternoon, a few minutes after 4 o'clock, while Mr. Jordan K. Piper, Superintendent of the Merchants Mill, was assisting in lowering by means of a tackle and fall, an empty machinery box from the fourth story of the tower of the mill, the box swung round and struck him in such a manner as to knock him out of the door, and he fell to the ground, a distance of about 45 feet. Mr. Jennings, the agent of the mill, being near by at the time, immediately hastened to his side, and heard him utter several times, in a faint voice, the words, "oh dear! oh dear!" The unfortunate man was at once removed to his residence, a few rods distant, but breathed his last almost immediately. He was in the 54th year of his age, and leaves a wife, two sons and a daughter. Funeral services were held at his late residence yesterday afternoon, at half past 5 o'clock, and this morning his remains were taken to Lewiston, Me., where he formerly resided.

Mr. Piper removed to this city about two years ago, and became Superintendent of the Merchants Mill. He was a very worthy man, and a good citizen, and was held in high esteem by all who enjoyed his acquaintance. The news of his sudden death, and the shocking manner in which it occurred, spread a gloom over our community, and was the subject of fitting remarks in some of our pulpits yesterday.

The Providence *Journal* of this morning, in noticing the sad event, says:

Mr. Piper was for many years a resident of Lewiston, Me., where he was well known, both in manufacturing and municipal circles. A few years previous to his leaving that city he was agent of the Lewiston Mills, and under his supervision the mills were enlarged to double their former capacity. He was active in city affairs, having served two years in the Common Council and one in the Board of Aldermen, and for many years an efficient member of the School Committee."

74.Article from the *Fall River Daily Evening News* reporting the death of Jordan K. Piper, a "sad accident." "The story … will appear a very strange one and perhaps would form a good plot for a modern mystery novel."

But after a few days and nights of worry, he walked into the bank – not the Fall River National, by the way – and asked the cashier to figure out how much he was liable for principal and interest to date. He gave his check with the remark that he never wanted to think of it again.

The story which I am now going to relate will appear a very strange one and perhaps would form a good plot for a modern mystery novel. Many years ago, the Superintendent of the Merchants Mills was a man named [*Jordan K.*] Piper (1818-1871), who lived in the little cottage at the south end of the mill. One day, the whole city was startled by the report that Mr. Piper had fallen from the fourth story of the mill and been instantly killed. Well I remember when his son [*either Willie F. (b.1859) or George M. Piper (b.1856)*] was called out of the school room to be told of the accident. More than thirty years afterward, a citizen who is now living told me that he had a queer story to tell me. A widow, formerly of Fall River, had become a nurse in a Boston Hospital, and a dying patient told her that he had worked for the Merchants Mills, and that there had been labor trouble and that he had pushed the Superintendent, a man named Piper, out of the open door in the fourth story and killed him.

At the time I was writing the financial news for the *Fall River Globe*, and told the story to Frank Kennedy, the editor; he immediately phoned the *Boston Globe*, of which he was the correspondent. They interviewed the nurse who confirmed the story so far as the confession of her patient was concerned. But, being the widow of a former well-known Fall River citizen, she obtained a promise from the *Boston Globe* that they would not publish the story because her name would, of course, appear prominently and, if any investigation was made, it would prove very embarrassing to her, and so the whole matter was dropped and will remain a mystery forever.

William Mason, who lived at 110 North Main Street in the house [*that is*] now the main building of the Quequechan Club, was one of the outstanding men of his time. A large, impressive figure, florid complexion, snow white hair and whiskers, which covered his chin and were kept carefully trimmed. He was always immaculately dressed: black cut-away coat, light trousers, patent-leather shoes, and fawn-colored spats. In summer, he wore a high white hat and always carried a gold-headed cane.

In the stress of the times of which I am speaking, he found it necessary to call a meeting of the creditors of a firm of which he was a partner at the office of James Madison Morton Sr., (1837-1923); present were a number of lawyers from out of the city and also accountants. [*According to his obituary, Mason "suffered reverses" as a result of the financial panic of*

75. Residence of William Mason, 110 North Main Street. The structure was later acquired by the Quequechan Club; incorporated into a larger structure, it formed the northern part of the club headquarters.

1873-74. A few years before his death, at which time he was associated with the firm of Stafford, Pierce & Mason, partners with Foster H. Stafford and Asabel T. Pierce, yarn manufacturers, he was again "involved in financial difficulties."]

The story of that meeting as related by one of the accountants follows:

Ten o'clock was the appointed time, the hour struck, and Mr. Mason did not appear ... five minutes, ten minutes, and the lawyers looked from one to the other, impatient at the delay. At about a quarter after the hour, the door slowly opened and this old gentleman, dressed as for a wedding, entered the room, cane in one hand and a small bag in the other. Looking the assembly over, he said: "Gentlemen, I owe you an apology for being late, but I did not sleep much last night. This morning, I called my wife [*née Emeline Frances Reed*] into my library and said, 'At ten o'clock, I am to meet my creditors. I have an insurance policy payable to you. We have lived well all these years and if you feel the way I do I would like you to assign this policy to my creditors so that I may deliver to them everything I have.'"

76. William Mason. He "delivered all of his assets absolutely, having retained them in his own name with no thought of any but his lawful creditors."

77. James Madison Morton Sr. A much esteemed jurist, he remarked in reference to William Mason's financial difficulties that, with one exception, this was the only case in his experience where a man of large means faced with the loss of his fortune had delivered all of his assets absolutely.

Slowly, he opened the bag, drew a paper from it, and said: "Gentlemen, here is a list of everything I own and here is the policy assigned to you." With one accord, those present rose to their feet and one by one grasped him by the hand unable to speak from emotion.

The gentleman who related this occurrence said that he never had witnessed so dramatic a scene, even upon the stage. Judge Morton remarked later that, with one exception, this was the only case in his experience where a man of large means faced with the loss of his fortune had delivered all of his assets absolutely, having retained them in his own name with no thought of any but his lawful creditors.

And Mr. Mason was appointed trustee of the estate by the creditors.

Linden Cook (1809-1884), who lived on Bedford Street and was the uncle of [*Brigadeer*] General Henry Clay Cook (1837-1916), was a large owner in the Robeson Mills on Hartwell Street, now the Luther Mills. He at one time accepted the treasurership of the Robeson Mills and was quite successful in his management. It was stated that the Board of Directors wished to grant him an increase in salary. He was a very large man and I never saw him sitting down in his office or without his hat on his head. He knew nothing of business forms and would call the bank messenger to one side to ask him how he should accept a draft or sign a legal document, speaking in a low tone so that his clerks would not become aware of his ignorance of business details. But, like many men, he had the trading instinct and knew how to make a good bargain.

The staid businessmen enjoyed their jokes and, if they could put something over on their associates, did not hesitate to do so.

Foster Hazard Stafford (1815-1891) had a very gruff manner and it was a common thing for treasurers and superintendents, if they had a persistent salesman or a young and fresh cotton broker, to send him to call upon Mr. Stafford, so that he was overrun with agents and drummers of all kinds. The word was passed from one to another of these dignified gentlemen who enjoyed it as a great joke. Mr. Stafford said nothing, but bided his time and returned the joke with interest.

He was president and agent of the Stafford Mills. He would hand all papers over to Mr. [*Shubael P.*] Lovell (1846-1882), his treasurer, and then enter into conversation with the messenger. On one occasion, when I was in the office, a finely dressed and extremely polite gentleman entered with a large folio under his arm. Asking Mr. Stafford if he was the president, he stated that he had a series of pictures of game and gaming scenes, the set selling for $300.00. Of course, he could only call upon those who appreciated art and had the means to purchase.

78. Foster Hazard Stafford. He "had a very gruff manner and it was a common thing for treasurers and superintendents, if they had a persistent salesman or a young and fresh cotton broker, to send him to call upon Mr. Stafford, so that he was overrun with agents and drummers of all kinds."

79. Walter Chaloner Durfee.

Mr. Stafford consented to look at them and they were certainly beautiful. However, he was not interested as a buyer. Thanking him for his courtesy, the agent asked if he could give him a few names of men of means who would be interested. Mr. Stafford said: "Yes, you go from here to the Wampanoag Mills and meet Mr. Walter C[*haloner*] Durfee, the treasurer; he is of a somewhat sporting disposition and you will have no trouble in selling him." The name was jotted down in a note book and others were asked for. Mr. Stafford again said: "Yes, you go down to the Shove Mills, over the line in Tiverton, [*Rhode Island*] and call for Mr. George Albert Chace (1844-1907); he is another sport, reckless with his money, and he will surely buy." This name went down in the note book, and another suggestion was requested. Again Mr. Stafford directed: "Go up north to the Narragansett Mills, call for Mr. James Waring (1821-1898) and, as soon as you get in conversation, call him by his first name, he will like that, and you won't have to spend much time with him – the sporty character of the pictures will surely appeal to him." This name was recorded and Mr. Stafford said: "Oh, yes, there is one more, in the center of the city; Mr. [*Azariah Shove*] Tripp (1826-1888) at the Metacomet National Bank. He is free with his money, greatly interested in art, and he will buy a set to put on his directors' table."

The agent was most profuse in his thanks and went on his way. Mr. Stafford looked at me and said: "I suppose I should call him back, he will be disappointed. But no, I won't, he will go no farther than the Wampanoag Mills."

Edmund Chase (1818-1883) was another strong and greatly esteemed citizen. He was a [*leather*] tanner located on Bedford Street at the foot of Rock Street; Third Street had not been cut through at that time. He was a large owner of mill stock and president of the Massasoit National Bank. Two nephews, Henry Buffington Slade Chase (1840-1914) and Stephen A. Chase (1839-1912), were his clerks.

When he built the brick mansion later occupied by Edward Brayton (1888-1980), his nephews planned to present him with a picture, suitably framed. It had been Mr. Chase's boast that nothing could be stolen from his factory, so perfect was his system of keeping stock. My father, a harness maker, bought his leather from Mr. Chase, and they were close friends.

The nephews proposed that they should steal the leather a little at a time and father was to make the frame. This was done and at the house-warming, picture and frame were presented to Mr. Chase with the information that the leather for the frame had been stolen by his clerks. The frame and cord with tassels attached is made entirely of leather. When the brick house was sold, the picture went to Stephen A. Chase, from him to his widow [*née Mary Elizabeth McCallum (1848-1916)*], and she gave it to the Christian Science Church, and it is now in the reading room of the Church at the corner of Rock and Pine Streets. It has changed to a deep mahogany color and the caretaker of the Church told me that, until I called, he had always supposed it was made of carved mahogany.

In writing an article of this kind, one figure after another rises in memory before ones vision. I suppose others present like myself could go on almost without end as thoughts of the past recur to them.

James E. Cunneen (1833-1914) – How many anecdotes could be related about him? Well I remember a convention held in the concert hall over Wordell and McGuire's store on Pleasant Street [*Marcus M. Wordell (1844-1912) and Thomas C. McGuire (b. c.1860), clothing and gents' furnishing goods*] to nominate a candidate for Mayor. After the preliminaries, nominations were called for. Mr. Cunneen arose in the center of the hall and, in his inimitable manner, gave this gem of oratory which I remember word for word: "Mr. Chairman, I have repeatedly importuned to run for Mayor of Fall River but I have peremptorily declined. I therefore, Mr. Chairman, move you the nomination of the Honorable Milton Reed [*1848-1932*] by unanimous acclamation."

William Durfee (1811-1901), "Ice Bill Durfee" – as he was called, to distinguish him from "Gas Bill Durfee," the treasurer of the Fall River Gas Works Company – was a familiar figure on Main Street. He owned the Richardson House property on the west side of North Main Street where the Mohican building and the Durfee Theater are now located [*in 1933*]. He always dressed well, but his attire was somewhat original. His hat was an old-fashioned silk beaver with a perfectly flat brim; I have never seen one like it before, or since. It was carefully brushed and ironed at all times. His suit was of heavy dark blue material, the same in summer and winter. To all appearances, his clothes were new and fitted him perfectly. His top boots were of heavy leather and carefully polished. The bottoms of his trousers had a V-shaped slit at the side so that they fitted perfectly over his massive boots.

At one time, when a friend asked him how he had acquired a severe cold, he said: "By standing on the Central Street crossing waiting for Nat [*Nathaniel C.*] Lucas (1824-1906) [*a hack driver*] to get by with his balky horses."

An artist once painted a picture of Mr. Durfee, which was very satisfactory to his family, but brought no comment from him. The artist asked for his opinion, as he wished his approval also. Mr. Durfee had

80. William "Ice Bill" Durfee. "He always dressed well, but his attire was somewhat original. His hat was an old-fashioned silk beaver with a perfectly flat brim; I have never seen one like it, or since. It was carefully brushed and ironed at all times. His suit was of a heavy dark blue material, the same in summer and winter. To all appearances, his clothes were new and fit him perfectly. His top boots were of heavy leather and carefully polished. The bottoms of his trousers had a V-shaped slit at the side so that they fitted perfectly over his massive boots."

endorsed quite heavily for friends, and it was necessary for him to visit the banks frequently. Looking out of the window, he said: "You go down to that bank across the street and show the picture to the cashier. If he says it is good, it is all right. He has seen more of me in the last six months than my family have."

Azariah S. Tripp, for many years cashier of the Metacomet National Bank, was perhaps the most able banker that Fall River has produced. He was very clear headed, a keen judge of human nature, and he frequently lent money to men whose social standing was not of the highest, and whose personal habits were not of the best, while refusing to give credit to men who posed as leading citizens or as the modern expression has it, super men. His stamp of approval from a banking standing point was based almost solely upon personal honor. Once a man had demonstrated his honesty and his determination to stand by his word and his obligation, he was assured of Mr. Tripp's support in financial matters. On the other hand, no matter how good the security might be, if the name signed to the note was not that of a man of whose integrity he was satisfied, he would not recommend the note to his directors. This was his rule: "If we have only the collateral, and that shrinks, we have nothing. If we have no collateral but a good name, we always have security."

The morning after he died [*in 1888*], Mr. Frank S. Stevens said: "We have lost a very able man. When we thought we had no solution for a financial problem and were ready to give up, Mr. Tripp always had some proposition which cleared the fog and renewed our courage."

Uncle Nat Horton [*Nathaniel Baker Horton (1821-1900)*] – "Rehoboth Horton" – who that ever knew him could forget the kindly spirit, the sympathy for the poor, and the dry wit that characterized his speech?

At a meeting of the stockholders of the old Robeson Mills, at which I was present, a proposition was put forward to increase the stock by an additional issue, the then present stockholders to subscribe for the new stock and pay cash for the same. Uncle Nat arose and opposed it for the reason that his sympathy was with the "widdys and orphans," a common expression with him. He feared that many of them would not be able to pay and might lose their holdings. Two gentlemen not renowned for their liberality or leniency towards their debtors announced that if any were not able to pay for the stock right away they would be pleased to take their notes with the stock as security. Uncle Nat slowly came to his feet, with the most painful expression imaginable on his face and said: "My sympathy with the 'widdys and orphans' is deeper than ever," and the proposition failed.

Robert Knight Remington, the founder of Borden & Remington [*dealers in calico printers', dyers', and woolen manufacturers' supplies*] will be remembered by all who knew him because of his personal charm and his many-sided character. Mr. Remington was a very handsome man, not of the effeminate type, large of figure, erect of carriage, and a face that radiated cheer, happiness, and love of his fellow men. But he could be as tender as a woman – the appeals of the suffering, the cares, the weaknesses of others, brought genuine sorrow to him. A story of misery, of misfortune, brought the ready tears to his eyes and his purse was always open to the poor and needy.

His interest in young men was the outstanding passion of his life and many a man grown now to middle and old age feels a debt of gratitude to him for the advice and guidance given to them by Mr. Remington. Many of you no doubt remember him as he appeared in the summer time, dressed in a white duck suit, starched like a dress shirt, immaculate linen, patent leather boots with soft enamel leather tops, and the inevitable high white hat. No man less handsome than he could have worn this costume without appearing a fop. But Mr. Remington never appeared as anything but a high-toned aristocratic gentleman.

He once compromised with his creditors and afterwards paid them in full with interest.

He purchased the Samuel Thaxter stone house [*in 1869, that was*] located on Columbia Street, had it taken apart, stone by stone, and reconstructed at the corner of Maple and Rock Streets. Afterwards, he sold it to David Anthony Brayton Sr. and [*at the time of this writing*] it is now occupied by [*his daughter*], Miss Elizabeth Hitchcock Brayton (1865-1935). [*Following her death, the residence was donated to the Fall River Historical Society by her nephew, David Anthony Brayton (1900-1975).*]

David Anthony Brayton Sr. (1824-1881) was always recognized as one of the leaders in cotton manufacturing. George H. Hawes, the leading cloth broker of the city, once stated that for clearness of mind, broad business view, fearlessness as to holding goods or selling in large quantities when he made up his mind to sell, he had never seen the equal of Mr. Brayton.

Hezekiah Anthony Brayton (1832-1908), his brother, of course made a great reputation as a manufacturer but, as an all-round businessman he exhibited unusual ability. He served as cashier of the First National Bank at one time, and the messenger boys soon discovered that he was a very sympathetic man, and ever willing to make their lot as pleasant as possible and encourage them to make the most of their lives. Almost immediately

81. David Anthony Brayton Sr. He "was always recognized as one of the leaders in cotton manufacturing [*and noted for*] clearness of mind [*and a*] broad business view."

82. Hezekiah Anthony Brayton. He "made a great reputation as a manufacturer [*and*] as an all-around businessman he exhibited universal ability."

after taking office, he objected to some methods of transacting business between banks which had prevailed for a long time, and insisted upon new and more up-to-date methods. He was right in the stand he took and would not budge until new rules were put into effect.

Mr. Brayton, at one time, was sitting in an office where he did a large amount of business; the telephone rang, a clerk answered, and the proprietor told him to tell the party he was not in. Mr. Brayton, in his impulsive way, jumped to his feet and demanded to know if they taught their clerks to lie, and if they were taught to lie to him. He stalked out of the office and it was a long time before he renewed his connection with the firm.

And now, off the record, as the lawyers phrase it.

Changing one word of the line from *The Bohemian Girl*: "For Memory is the only thing that grief can call its own." We sometimes feel "That Memory is the only thing that age can call its own." [*The Bohemian Girl is an opera in three acts written by Michael William Balfe (1808-1870), with a libretto by Alfred Bunn (1796-1860), based on a story by Cervantes. It was first produced at London's Drury Lane Theatre in November of 1843.*]

My friends, this is not so.

Often, I have stood at the corner where the old bank building was located and, in memory, only have seen the men and women of the time of which I have spoken, and their associates, as strong and sturdy as they were. Slowly, they approached, slowly they passed from my vision. And then I turned from the unreal to the real and see the sons and grandsons, the daughters and grand-daughters, descendants of these men and women, heirs to a priceless heritage, who, whatever happened to Fall River, never faltered, and I have the hope, yes, the certainty, that the city will carry on, blessed by heaven and glorified by its memories.

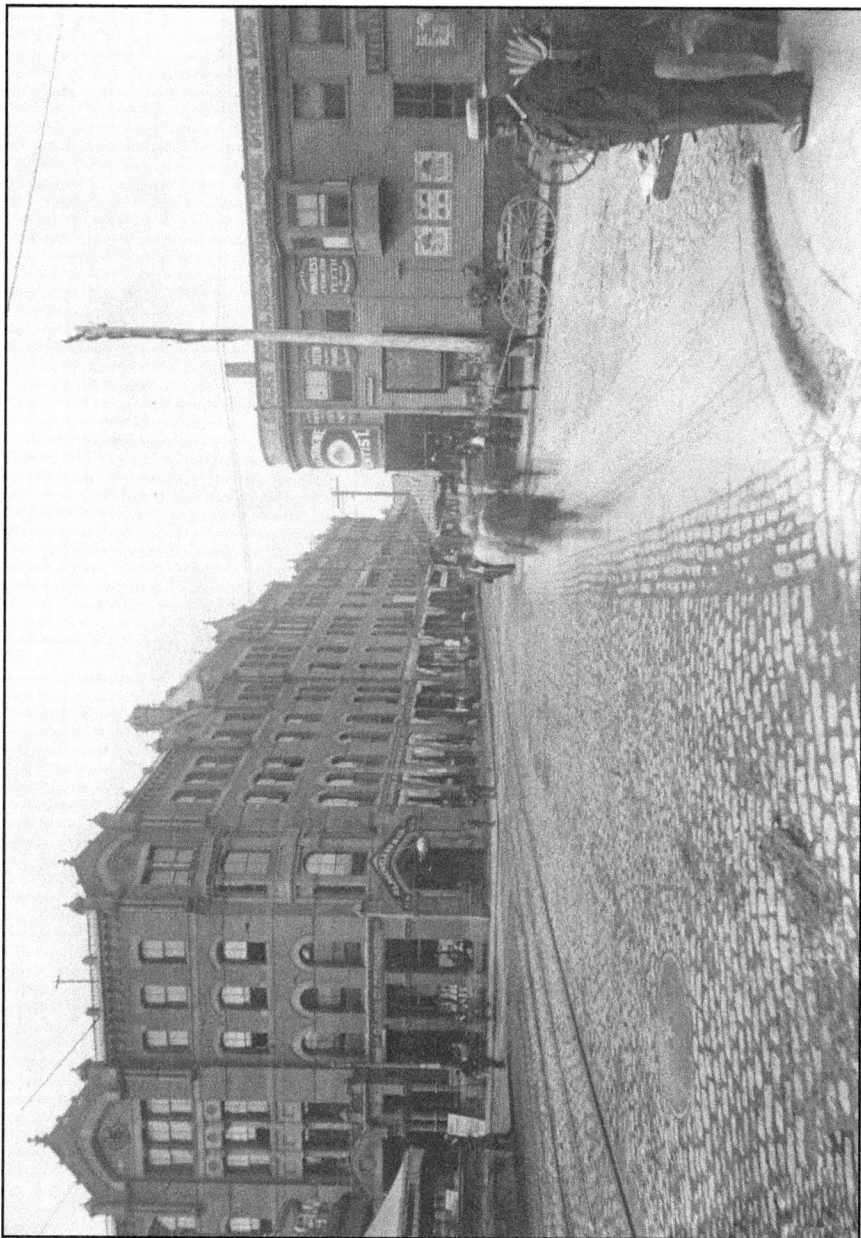

83. View looking south from the corner of North Main and Central Streets, facing South Main Street. "Often, I have stood at the corner where the old bank was located and, in memory, only have seen the men and women of the time of which I have spoken."

Bibliography

Published works:

Adjutant General, compiler. *Massachusetts Soldiers, Sailors, and Marines in the Civil War, Vols. I – VIII.* Norwood, Massachusetts: The Norwood Press, 1932.

American Newspaper Annual; Philadelphia, Pennsylvania; N. W. Ayer & Son, 1882.

Buckley, Rev. Michael Bernard. *Diary of a Tour in America.* Dublin, Ireland: Sealy, Bryers & Walker, 1889.

Case, C.V. *Genealogical Record of the Chace and Hathaway Families from 1630-1900.* Ashtabula, Ohio: T.E. Wilson Co.

Forbes, A. and J.W. Greene. *The Rich Men of Massachusetts.* Boston, Massachusetts: W.V. Spencer, 1851.

Hurd, D. Hamilton, ed. *History of Bristol County, Massachusetts.* Philadelphia, Pennsylvania: J.W. Lewis & Co., 1883.

Hutt, Frank Walcott, ed. *A History of Bristol County, Massachusetts, Vols. 1 – 3.* New York and Chicago: Lewis Historical Publishing Co., Inc., 1924.

Kelland, Clarence Budington. "Scattergood Moves to Adjourn." *American Magazine*, Volume LXXXIX, January 1920 – June 1920. New York, New York: The Crowell Publishing Company.

Lynch, Capt. Thomas E. *History of the Fire Department of Fall River, Mass.* Fall River, Massachusetts: Almy & Milne, 1896.

Martins, Michael and D.A. Binette. *Parallel Lives: A Social History of Lizzie A. Borden and Her Fall River.* Fall River: Fall River Historical Society Press, 2010.

Peirce, Ebenezer W. *The Peirce Family of the Old Colony.* Boston, Massachusetts: David Clapp and Son, 1870.

Report of the Watuppa Water Board to the City Council, January 1, 1875.
 Fall River, Massachusetts: Fiske & Monroe, Steam Book & Job
 Printers, 1875.

Representative Men and Old Families of Southeastern Massachusetts,
 Vols. 1 – 3. Chicago, Illinois: J.H. Beers & Co., 1912.

Silvia, Philip T. Jr., Ph.D. *Victorian Vistas: Fall River 1865-1885.* Fall
 River, Massachusetts: R.E. Smith Co., 1987.

Weld, Hattie. *Historical and Genealogical Record of Richard and Joan*
 Borden. Albany, New York: Joe Munsell's Sons, 1899.

Directories:

Fall River City Directory, 1853-1857. Boston, MA: George Adams.

Fall River City Directory, 1859-1864. Boston, MA: Adams, Sampson & Co.

Fall River City Directory, 1866-1884. Boston, MA: Sampson, Davenport &
 Co.

Fall River City Directory, 1885-1900. Boston, MA: Sampson, Murdock &
 Co.

Ephemera:

Foster, Stephen Collins. "Massa's In De Cold Ground." New York, New
 York: Firth, Pond & Company, 1852.

Foster, Stephen Collins; "Old Black Joe"; New York, New York, Firth, Pond
 & Company, 1860.

Geoghegan, Joseph George; "Down In A Coal Mine"; Jersey City, New
 Jersey, W. H. Ewald & Brothers, 1872.

Newspapers:

Fall River Daily Evening News
Fall River Daily Globe
Fall River Daily Herald
Fall River Herald News
Providence Journal

About the Fall River Historical Society

Incorporated in 1921, Fall River Historical Society (FRHS), a public charity, is the oldest cultural institution in the city that is dedicated to collecting and exhibiting artifacts and archival material relative to the history and multi-cultural people of Fall River. We serve the public through guided tours, exhibitions, educational programs, publications, and cultural events, and frequently partner with the city and other non-profit organizations in presenting events for the benefit of the community. The FRHS is recognized in the Greater Fall River area as a leading provider of innovative historical and cultural programming.

The FRHS was founded in 1921 by a group of individuals intent on preserving the history of Fall River, once an important textile center with the distinction of being one of the world's largest producer of cotton cloth. Since its incorporation, the organization has been actively acquiring material pertaining to the city's history and has amassed a vast collection, the majority of which is accompanied by detailed provenance.

A tragic set-back occurred on the evening of February 2, 1928, when a devastating conflagration destroyed a large section of the Fall River business district. Among the victims, and situated almost in the center of the burned out area, was the supposedly fire-proof Buffington Building, which housed the office and exhibition room of the FRHS. The entire collection was lost, except for a selection of important items stored in a safe, which survived the inferno unscathed. Undaunted, the organization immediately resumed gathering material, thereby forming the nucleus of the collection as it exists today.

The diverse collections of the FRHS continue to grow in all categories, and include: Americana; Costumes and Accessories; Decorative Arts; Ephemera; Fall River Textile Industry; Furniture; Local History; Manuscripts; Maritime; Paintings, Drawings, and Sculpture, 19th Century;

Paintings, Drawings, and Sculpture, 20th Century and Contemporary; and Photographs. Items from our collections have been loaned for exhibition at institutions nationwide.

The vast majority of the FRHS's holdings are acquired by gift. In addition, we seek out and purchase items of historical importance through the generosity of private donors and donations made to our Acquisition Fund.

The FRHS has been collecting archival and library material pertaining to Fall River history since its incorporation, with examples dating from the late-seventeenth to the mid-twentieth century; the holdings, which are ever-growing, constitute the largest collection of its type extant in the city. In 2009, the library and archive was designated The Charlton Library of Fall River History in recognition of the Ida S. Charlton Charity Fund, which sponsored the expansion and refitting of the facility and the conservation of a portion of the Society's holdings. The Fund made an additional contribution in 2012, allowing further expansion and, in 2016, a generous grant from the Earle P. Charlton Jr. Charity Fund made advanced development possible.

The library, which is non-circulating, houses an important research collection of books, pamphlets, periodicals, and reference materials. Published material includes biographies, *Fall River City Directories*, local authors, genealogy, family histories, memoirs, municipal documents, periodicals, and regional histories pertinent to the city of Fall River, as well as city, county, economic, ethnic, industrial, maritime, military, Native American, political, and social histories. Select baptismal, business, church, and probate records are available, as are a large number of unpublished papers and manuscripts. Materials are added to the library on a regular basis.

Holdings include a microfilm collection containing in excess of 100,000 issues of 19th and 20th century Fall River newspapers, with the earliest dating to 1858, as well as scrapbooks compiled by private individuals and organizations. The Society's manuscript collection contains thousands of documents, including family and personal papers, corporate and legal documents, business records, church records, diaries, and journals. Also available is the most extensive collection of Fall River textile mill records and manuscripts in existence.

The photograph collection contains thousands of examples, and is widely recognized as the most comprehensive assemblage of its type pertaining to Fall River. With images dating from the dawn of photography to the mid-20th century, the collection documents the changing landscape of the city's public and private spaces, its cultural development, and the faces of its inhabitants.

The FRHS is recognized, world-wide, as the central repository for material pertaining to the infamous 1892 Borden Murder Case and the life of Lizzie Andrew Borden (1860-1927), who was tried and acquitted for that heinous crime. The Borden collections, which are unsurpassed, include original trial exhibits, photographs, and the most significant primary source material extant.

The FRHS operates Fall River Historical Society Press, dedicated to publishing works on a wide range of historical topics, with all proceeds benefiting the organization.

For more information about Fall River Historical Society, visit our website at fallriverhistorical.org, or contact us at 508-679-1071.

ACKNOWLEDGMENTS

The Fall River Historical Society is deeply indebted to Nancy A. Teasdale, who has voluntarily spent untold hours transcribing the original manuscript of this and numerous other papers that were presented at society meetings in decades past. Her diligent perseverance, without which the *Discourses on History* series would not be possible, is hereby gratefully acknowledged.

Special thanks to the following for their research and assistance in the preparation of this volume:

Caroline H. Aubin
Danielle Cabral
Kathryn S. Croan
Martha Burrell Foster
Stefani Koorey, PhD
Constance C. Mendes
William A. Moniz
David Roseberry
Philip T. Silvia Jr. PhD
Nancy A. Teasdale
Cynthia Tobojka

Index

by Stefani Koorey, PhD

Entries are arranged in word-by-word order, using the *Chicago Manual of Style, 16th Edition*. References to page numbers for illustrations are indicated by numerals in bold type.

All females are listed by their last known surname, followed in parentheses by maiden name, with cross-references provided from maiden name for ease of location. In places where maiden surnames are unknown, first names are provided. All placenames, including streets, companies, churches, and schools, are located in Fall River, Massachusetts, unless specifically noted.

NOTES

NOTES

* 9 7 8 0 9 6 4 1 2 4 8 0 6 *